Hot Bass Flies

Patterns & Tactics from the Experts

Deke Meyer

Hot Bass Flies

Patterns & Tactics from the Experts

Deke Meyer

Frank Amato
PORTLAND

Dedication

Dedicated to all fly-flingers for bass, be they known or unknown.

*Tip for modifying the action of foam poppers and sliders: drill
a small hole, insert some lead wire, glue in place. The
additional weight makes the foam head burrow
into the water on the retrieve, allowing for
more fly gyrations while not
moving it very far.*

Frank Amato Publications, Inc.

P.O. Box 82112, Portland, Oregon 97282

503·653·8108 • www.amatobooks.com

All photographs by the author unless otherwise noted.
All fly plate photographs by Jim Schollmeyer
Book & Cover Design: Kathy Johnson

Printed in Hong Kong

Softbound ISBN: 1-57188-285-5 • UPC: 0-81127-00103-3
Spiral Hardbound ISBN: 1-57188-286-3 • UPC: 0-81127-00104-0

1 3 5 7 9 10 8 6 4 2

Contents

When pigs fly...

Fly-fishing for bass can be a lifelong love affair.

Hot Bass Flies

Introduction

Bass are fun because they readily take flies of many sorts and under widely varied conditions.

Fly fishing for bass is hotter than ever. Bass thrive from Mexico to Canada, from the East to the West coast, in ponds and lakes, coves and creeks, reservoirs and streams. As prime game fish and superior predators, bass readily attack flies, whether topwater poppers or divers, subsurface streamers or crayfish, wiggling worms or other crawly critters.

Bass flies are hotter than ever, too. Combining traditional fur, feathers and rubber legs with modern synthetics, innovative designers have developed bass flies that wiggle and waggle, spin and dart, pop and gurgle, slink and undulate, all of which drive bass wild. If you don't tie flies, commercial sources for purchasing flies and/or materials are listed on page 130.

Effective weedguard designs allow you to fly fish for bass in dense cover, under lily pads, in submerged trees or brush, or anywhere you find bass, which includes dropping your fly alongside that sunken '47 Ford where you might catch a bass big enough to need a license plate.

Experts will tell you how they catch bass, from the ponds in Central Park, New York City, to the cypress swamps in the Carolinas, to the Florida Everglades, to the 'gator country in Georgia, to the stock tanks in Texas, to the clear, finesse-style waters in California, to prime smallmouth habitat in Oregon.

Parker's Bat
(Pete Parker)

Hook: Daiichi 2461, size 4/0
Thread: Dynacord Super Thread or Kevlar
Body: Natural deer hair
Wings: Natural deer hair; stiffened with Duco Household Cement
Head: Brown deer hair
Ears: Brown deer hair; stiffened with Duco Household Cement
Eyes: Doll eyes, black on yellow
Eye Glue: Hot Stuff Super T
Notes: Pete Parker of Indian Hills, Colorado says, "I have given away a hundred of these flies through the years and to my knowledge no one has caught a fish on one. I certainly have not. However, I have had a great deal of

fun with this fly. I call it my "patch" fly. When I hike into Cheeseman Canyon on the South Platte River in Colorado, where trout fishing is great but fly size 22's to 26's are the rule, I put a Bat Fly on my vest patch. When I pass other anglers I mutter The Bat is really working today."

Because of the visual thrill, catching bass on a popper is probably the most fun.

Hot Bass Flies

Poppers

The method is the madness—it's more fun to catch bass on a fly rod than any other way. And a popper is the most fun because when the bass attacks your popper, you see it happen. It's so exciting that you'll be lucky not to rip the popper right out of the fish's mouth.

Dating back to early in the 20th century, the first hard poppers were made with cork heads, with the hook further decorated with fur and feathers. Cork still makes for a fine popper, although good-quality cork can be hard to find. Plastic or soft-foam poppers are more common because of availability of materials and they're less trouble to make. Simply super glue them on a hook, tie on some feathers and you're ready to go.

Deer-hair poppers also date back to roughly the same time, and still remain popular because tiers like to spin on deer hair, then add feathers and eyes. Varying the color of the hair and creative trimming adds to the charm of this traditional popper. And deer-hair poppers catch bass.

If you tie your own poppers you can create whatever you want. However, for fishing, sometimes simple is better. More than once I've been out with older, experienced fly-rodders who fish with a minimalist popper, one with a painted cork head, no eyes, and a few feathers or a tuft of fur for the tail. That's it. And they would often outfish my more complicated poppers because they concentrated on presentation. They were tuned in to where they cast the popper, how they retrieved it, and how fast they retrieved it. They would vary how long they let the popper sit, the amount of pop they imparted to it and the amount of time between pops, until the bass told them they liked it by striking their popper. Those popper maestros would make that popper spurt and strut, stand on its toes and bury its face, gurgle and spit, and anything else they could think of.

So I learned that instead of worrying about how my popper was dressed, I was better off varying my retrieve until I started catching fish.

Traditionally, poppers and many other bass flies were tied on the Mustad 3366, and many tiers still prefer that hook. However, advances in chemical sharpening of hooks and improved computer-driven metallurgy now allows tiers to choose from a vast array of higher-quality hooks from Mustad, Tiemco, Daiichi, and others.

For popper fishing, the only limiting factor is that the bass must be in relatively shallow water, which means spring and fall, or early morning and late evening in the summer. A summer rain storm can move bass to the shallows looking for prey because bass prefer the lower light of the cloud cover and the cooler water temperature can rev them up. Also, bass will respond to a popper from farther away if the water is clear. In off-color water, try casting your popper to a good spot several times before moving on—it may take more than one cast for the bass to tune in on your popper.

Popper Dropper

This variation is one that works in murky water when you want to call bass to your popper, but they don't want to hit it. In shallow water where bass are chasing prey, they may be reluctant to hit your popper, especially if the water is worked with poppers regularly.

To make the dropper, (page 11) simply attach an 18- to 24-inch length of tippet material to the bend of the popper hook with an improved clinch knot (or Trilene knot with braided material), (page 61) then tie on a dropper fly.

You can use almost any subsurface fly, but a weight-forward style that mimics a baitfish or baby bass or bluegill works best. By weight-forward, I mean a fly with weight on its front half, so that when you pull the popper, the dropper fly lifts up and forward, then when the popper rests, the dropper drifts back down, head-first. This up-and-down jigging motion of the dropper mimics a wounded baitfish, ready prey for bass.

The popper not only attracts shallow feeding fish, but acts as a strike indicator. Sure, sometimes bass will attack the dropper fly with vigor, but most subsurface strikes are more subtle, imparting a mere twitch to the popper as the bass slides up and inhales the dropper. The popper as strike indicator is very effective in turbid water.

The main drawback to this system is the tangles you get when casting two flies of varying weight and air resistance. The best course is to slow down your backcast and forward delivery, and open up the casting loop. Obviously, you won't be casting as far, so you'll need to get closer to the fish and concentrate on presentation.

As a bonus with the popper-dropper setup, you'll sometimes get a bass to nail the popper.

Ben's Balsa Popper
(Ben Wise)

Hook: Mustad popper hook, size 10
Thread: White
Tail: Brown calf tail
Collar: Grizzly hackle, optional
Body: Balsa painted brown, painted eye optional
Notes: I fished with Ben Wise at Westlake, California in July, 1992. I came prepared with a full armada of high-tech rods, hot-rod reels, the latest in lines, and piles of intricate bass flies. In spite of which, Ben taught me a valuable lesson. Sitting in the back of his aluminum boat powered by an electric motor, he fished with a glass fly rod, Pflueger Medalist reel, floating fly line that was once white but had faded and cracked to brown, a short leader with a stout tippet, and a simple, brown balsa popper. (His didn't have a hackle collar or painted eye—the one shown is a fancy version.)

Being the guest, I sat in front and had first shot at

the fish. The lesson: snicking his little popper more accurately into bassy pockets and closer to structure, Ben easily outfished me both in numbers and size of fish—fancy gear and flies are less important than accuracy and presentation. We didn't catch anything of size because the lake had just been treated with herbicide the day before, but Ben has taken bass to six pounds in the water we were fishing, on his simple popper.

Bouldin's Frog Popper
(Brooks Bouldin)

Hook: Stinger, size 10
Tail: Grizzly hackle, two pair, yellow, olive; yellow marabou
Body: Cork, painted, froggie
Collar: Grizzly hackle, yellow, olive
Eyes: Painted
Weedguard: Mason hard mono 20-pound, horse-shoe shape
Notes: An exquisite example of a traditional cork popper executed by Brooks Bouldin of Houston, Texas, who introduced Kevlar tying thread to fly fishermen.

Many consider the horseshoe style of weedguard more effective than the standard mono loop weedguard.

Burk's Poppin' Shad
(Andy Burk)

Hook: Stinger, size 2
Tail: Marabou, Krystal Flash
Body: Deer hair, pearlescent glitter on bottom
Eyes: Molded epoxy eye with pupil
Weedguard: Mason hard monofilament, 20-pound
Notes: Colors include fire tiger, gray, olive with pearl belly, red with pearl belly and purple with pearl belly. Andy Burk of Reno, Nevada devised this fly for the spotted bass in Lake Shasta in Northern California,

which feed heavily on shad. Andy spins the hair in his poppers so tight, they almost seem like they're made of foam or some other solid material.

Andy says, "A great method for fishing over large schools of shad is to cast minnow-shaped poppers with pearlescent bellies into the school. This method of surface fishing works best when bass are feeding aggressively, and you see fish boiling and chasing shad at the surface. I've found it best to cast the popper into the

fray and pop it rapidly several times just after it hits the water.

"This imitates a shad that is fleeing and then gives up. Bass usually hit during the pauses. Sometimes the strike is so violent it knocks the popper clear out of the water and away from the fish's mouth. If this happens the best tactic is to start your popping retrieve again—fish will often come back after a shad they missed on the first try."

Popper-Dropper Rig

ANDY BURK

Attach 18- to 24-inch length of tippet material to the bend of the popper hook with an improved clinch knot (or Trilene knot with braided material), then tie on a dropper fly.

Burk's Green Swamp Frog
(Andy Burk)

Hook: Stinger, size 2
Legs: Tied silicone strands, pumpkin, olive, pearl
Body: Deer hair
Eyes: Molded epoxy
Weedguard: Mason hard mono, 20-pound

Chappie's Pencil Popper
(George "Chappie" Chapman)

Hook: Mustad popper hook, long-shank saltwater, size 6
Thread: Fluorescent red
Tail: Frayed ends, pearlescent Mylar tubing
Collar: Grizzly hackle, optional
Body: Pearlescent Mylar tubing, frayed ends in front, over tapered balsa painted red
Eyes: Painted, large black pupil on yellow
Notes: George Chapman of Woodland Hills, California showed me his own variation of the traditional red/white pencil popper when I fished with him in July, 1992. (The bass at Oso Reservoir were tough, although we caught a few.) Innovative ideas include Mylar tubing

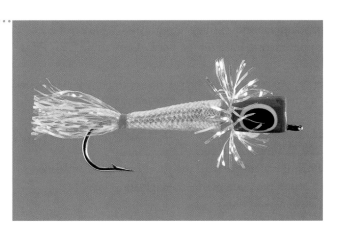

over a tapered balsa core, the frayed ends at the front of the tubing suggest the twitching dorsal and pectoral fins of a struggling, wounded baitfish.

Daubert's Frog
(Captain Ken Daubert)

Hook: Hook-up-front system
Body: A combination of foam and latex
Legs: Silicone
Notes: A saltwater and bass guide, Captain Ken Daubert of Silver Springs, Florida says, "Made of foam and a combination of latexes, this bug can be built to size for various line weights—you can make bullfrogs to spring peepers. As the frog is pulled forward on a sink-tip line, it dives just below the surface with the legs sweeping backward in a kicking motion. When the frog stops and comes to rest, the legs sweep forward and return to their position out to the sides, ready for another kick. It can be popped on the surface lightly or loudly. It often gets exploded on while sitting at rest for long periods or just jiggling a toe."

An originator of the Banjo Minnow Fishing System, Ken says, "The hook-up-front system is superior to standard hooks on flies because the hook point is the first thing that contacts the fish's mouth when the hook is set. It is also more convenient for changing lures, and it

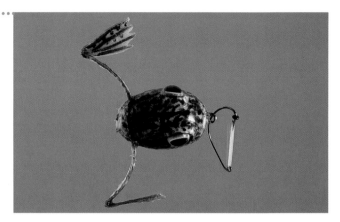

even saves leader tippets because it is not necessary to cut the hook off when you want to change flies. Also, you can store the flies in your shirt pocket without threat of getting hooked since there is no hook in the actual fly until you place the eye of the fly over your hook-point and slip it past the barb, securing it by placing a rubber O-ring over the hook-point and also pushing it down past the barb. Weight can be added by simply wrapping some lead wire around the modified kahle hook shank. You can attach the tiny rubber band weedguard to make your fly totally weedless."

Dave's Foam Hula Popper
(Dave Rabe)

Hook: Kink shank popper, size 1/0
Tail: Black rubber strands
Body: Black foam
Head: Black foam
Eyes: Solid plastic, black on yellow
Notes: From Milford, Ohio, this is the all-black rendition of Dave's version of that famous lure, the Hula Popper. He also likes a chartreuse body. He says, "The durability combined with the productivity of this fly makes it my absolute favorite for largemouth bass." (Notice a bit of tippet material still on the hook? Dave says, "This fly is

responsible for 43 bass from 1/2 pound to 8 1/2 pounds, it's very durable."

Earhart's Ultimate Popper
(Vann Earhart)

Hook: Mustad kink popper hook, size 1
Tail: White badger hackle tips
Body: Foam; white with gray back, red belly and face spot, rear side black spots, glitter
Collar: Black hackle
Eyes: Painted, black on yellow on white on black
Notes: A gorgeous example of the modern hard-foam popper, this is just one of dozens of versions. Vann says, "Our lures are all hand made and hand painted, even the eyes." Available wholesale from Ultimate Poppers (see Sources, page 130).

EdgeWater's Boilermaker
(EdgeWater)

Hook: Saltwater long shank, sizes 1/0-3/0
Tail: Bucktail, Krystal Flash
Body: Foam
Eyes: Solid plastic, black on yellow
Notes: This is the peppermint version. Although that color is no longer available, these are: yellow, white, black, chartreuse, white/red, blue, purple. The Rattle N Pop includes an enclosed rattle. Available from EdgeWater (see Sources, page 130).

EdgeWater's Chugger
(EdgeWater)

Hook: Stinger, sizes 10-1/0
Tail: Hackle, Krystal Flash
Collar: Hackle
Body: Foam
Legs: Rubber
Eyes: Doll eyes, black on white
Weedguard: Plastic-covered wire loops Available from EdgeWater (see Sources, page 130).
Notes: This is the white version. Others are yellow, blue, black, chartreuse, white/red, purple.

In his book, *Bassin' with a Fly Rod*, 1994, Jack Ellis says, "Bugs (or chuggers as we say in Texas) are by far the most widely used bass flies and the easiest to fish. I

would guess that the vast majority of fly-rod largemouth are taken on bugs. Whether constructed of deer hair, cork, wood, foam or hard plastic, all chuggers float and make varying degrees of commotion when retrieved."

EdgeWater's Pencil Popper
(EdgeWater)

Hook: Saltwater long shank, sizes 1/0 and 2/0
Tail: Marabou, Flashabou
Body: Foam
Eyes: Solid plastic, black on yellow
Notes: This is the chartreuse version. Others are yellow, white, black, purple, blue. Shorter versions are the Stretch and Dinks. Available from EdgeWater (see Sources, page 130.

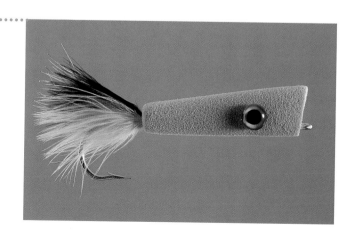

Ellis Bunny Foo-Foo Popper
(Joe Ellis)

Hook: Mustad long-shank stainless steel popper hook, size 1/0

Tail: Two rabbit strips , olive, white; pearl Krystal Flash

Body: EdgeWater 5/8 in foam cone, reversed; permanent marker, olive

Eyes: Doll eyes, black on white

Notes: This is the olive version. Joe Ellis of Cincinnati, Ohio also ties a black over white. The rabbit strips are tied down Matuka-style, hide to hide, fur-out.

Fluter
(Doug Swisher and Bob Marvin)

Hook: Stainless, long shank, sizes 1/0 and 3/0

Tail: Yellow bucktail; pearl Flashabou

Body: Foam, specially grooved

Notes: With a head that is fluted, or carved with long, rounded grooves, this fly is capable of spouting water when jerked on the retrieve. Originally designed for snook and other saltwater predators by Doug Swisher and Captain Bob Marvin of Naples, Florida, this is the chartreuse version; others include yellow, black, blue, white. Available from Doug Swisher, Edgewater and Larry Tullis, (see Sources, page 130).

Gaines's Bass King
(Gaines/Phillips)

Hook: Mustad bass popper, size 1/0

Tail: Grizzly hackle, yellow

Body: Cork, black with yellow stripes

Legs: White rubber

Collar: Yellow and black hackle

Eyes: Painted, black on red

Notes: Built in Gaines, Pennsylvania, this is a fine example of the traditional cork popper. This is the Bass King version; there are dozens of others. Gaines/Phillips still makes their poppers and sliders from cork although quality cork is difficult to obtain. Available retail from Cortland and wholesale from Gaines (see Sources, page 130).

In his *Book of the Black Bass*, 1881, 1923, James Henshall wrote, "The first bass bugs that I remember were made and sent to me during the World's Fair at Chicago, 1893. They were made from plump, buoyant bodies, dressed with silk floss and feathers, and with long wings, hackles, tails, and streamers of prismatic hues."

He quoted a letter from B.F. Wilder:

"In 1911, Mr. Louis Adams of New York gave me a cork bug, tied by himself or to his order. It was extremely attractive, but due to faults in construction it was hard to hook the fish that struck it.

"During that summer I improved the bug. I changed the shape and balance of the body, thus making it always float with the hook down, and I securely anchored the hook in the cork body by means of a sheet-steel fin soldered on the hook-shank. The resulting bug was as attractive as those tied by Mr. Adams, and it was now possible to hook the greater portion of the striking fish. But the changes I made were only improvements; Mr. Adams was the inventor.

"In 1912 I used this cork bug in Maine and taught Mr. James True of Norway, Maine, how to tie it. During 1913 he made and sold hundreds of bugs."

Historically, the first cork flies consisted of feathers or hair strapped onto cork with lashings of thread. Interestingly enough, no difference was drawn between flat-face or cone-face cork flies. Poppers or sliders were not mentioned, they were all just called bugs.

Galloway's Blue Foamin' Glitch Bug
(Bill Galloway)

Hook: Mustad 3366, sizes 1/0 to 2
Tail: Grizzly hackle; pearl Krystal Flash
Rear Collar: Grizzly hackle
Body: Pearl Crystal Chenille
Shellback: White foam; hood, permanent marker, blue
Legs: White round rubber
Weedguard: Mason hard mono 20-pound
Notes: This is the blue version. Others are purple, red, yellow. A bass guide out of Pyror, Oklahoma, Bill's approach is to use "large silhouette bass bugs that weigh very little, that cast well, and you can use light rods."

Gammel's Weed Runner Chartreuse Popper
(Bill Gammel)

Hook: Stinger, size 1/0
Tail: Chartreuse hackle; chartreuse Krystal Flash
Body: Chartreuse chenille palmered with chartreuse hackle
Legs: Round rubber, chartreuse, white
Wing: White closed-cell foam
Head: White closed-cell foam (can use EdgeWater Dink foam heads)
Weedguard: Notch in the foam wing
Notes: This is the chartreuse version. Others are frog, black, purple, white, yellow. If the foam doesn't sit tight against the hook point, Bill suggests holding the foam guard up, above the hook, then putting super glue on the top part where the foam hinges. When the glue dries it reinforces the bend in the foam, so that when you place it back under the hook point, the foam is under tension and will stay up against the point, making it weedless but not fishless.

He says, "When the fish are sucked back up in the grass, I throw it out over the tops of the grass beds and just bring it straight back to me. The bass that are hanging out in the cool shadows down below the matted surface will blow up through it and take the bug." (See Gammel's Weedrunner Slider, page 130.)

Gerbubble Bug
(Tom Loving)

Hook: Stinger, size 10
Tail: White marabou; splayed grizzly hackle tips
Collar: Grizzly hackle
Body: Spun deer hair, green, white
Legs: Grizzly hackle radiating out sideways
Eyes: Optional, doll eyes
Weedguard: Mason hard mono 20-pound
Notes: From Bridgeport, Texas, this is Bill Munn's version of a classic created in the 1920s by Tom Loving. Originally a cork or balsa fly, as shown in a color plate in John Alden Knight's book *Black Bass*, 1949, it was popularized by Joe Brooks.

Loving and Brooks both lived in Baltimore, Maryland and often fished together. In his book, *Complete Book of Fly Fishing*, 1958, 1968, Brooks wrote, "The Gerbubble bug picks up lightly, pops well, sits low in the water, and the fringe-like hackles on the sides and the flirting tail make it a potent bit of medicine for bass. Loving tied it on a No. 2/0 hook with cork body 9/16

inches high, 11/16 inches wide and 7/8 inches long. He painted his bugs an overall brown with red, white or yellow tiny circles or dots here and there; or all white, or all yellow, with the same added small eyes and circles, and matching feathers. This makes the bug look more natural than some of the bright colors painted on many bugs, and which I think are designed to dazzle the angler rather than the bass."

Dave Whitlock wrote about his deer-hair version in *The Fly-Tyer's Almanac*, Boyle and Whitlock, 1975.

Mark's Fire Tiger Maribug
(Mark Sturtevant)

Hook: Mustad 3366
Thread: Hot orange flat waxed nylon
Tail: Fluorescent orange marabou; black Flashabou
Skirt: Chartreuse Estaz
Head: Fluorescent chartreuse, black, fluorescent orange deer belly hair
Notes: Mark Sturtevant of Scotland, Pennsylvania says, "The Maribug is a great, simple, little fly that will pop quietly when twitched, with a following wiggle provided by the marabou tail. It catches a lot of bass in all sizes. I vary the color banding and head shape somewhat on these flies to achieve louder or softer pops and different visibility when fishing (orange in front is more visible in bright sunlight, chartreuse/lime is more visible in dim light—to the angler).

"During my tournament and guiding days I kept up on all the new technology of pro bass fishing. One big item was Dr. Loren Hill's Color-C-Lec-Tor device. This gadget confirmed the colors I had found most effective

by long experience on the water. It seems that these fluorescent colors and black cover a wide range of water clarity conditions, according to Hill's research. I have found that the effectiveness of Fire Tiger colored lures do indeed correspond with the clarity conditions indicated by Dr. Hill's device. So, depending upon your individual perspective, there is a scientific basis for why Fire Tiger works so well under so many conditions. I know bass like it!"

Mason's Aerofly
(Renny Mason)

Hook: Straight-eye hook
Body: Twisted chenille palmered with hackle
Wing: Yarn
Head: Foam over a hollow plastic tube
Notes: This is one of the black versions. There are six other versions, as well as a marabou series. Renny Mason of Bremerton, Washington says, "The Aerofly is a tube fly that will chug, dive, pop up and blow bubbles. It's important to use a hook that fits the tube. The hook must have an eye that can be pushed slightly into the nylon tube, just enough to hold it in place. You can customize the Aerofly by threading rubber legs or Krystal Flash through the foam or add doll eyes. (Renny recommends Seal All from the local auto parts store as an adhesive.) You can shade it with a felt pen." (If the permanent marker bleeds on the foam, use fabric paint.)

Peck's Popper
(Accardo/Peck's)

Hook: Mustad bass popper, size 1/0
Tail: Grizzly hackle, yellow
Body: Cork, frog coloration
Legs: White rubber
Collar: Grizzly hackle, yellow
Eyes: Painted, black on red
Notes: Built in Baton Rouge, Louisiana, this is a fine example of the traditional cork popper. This is the Special Popping Minnow version in frog colors; there are dozens of others. According to Tony Accardo, in 1920 E.H. "Peck" Peckinpaugh of Chattanooga, Tennessee founded his cork popper manufacturing company and began applying for patents in 1922. He is considered the father of the cork popper (although earlier designs had cork bodies, they were called feather minnows and were slider-shaped). Peck's designs still work: on March 25, 1984, Robert M. Ekker landed a 12-pound, 9-ounce largemouth bass on a size 4 Peck's Popper on Lake Tsala in Apopka, Florida that still stands as the IGFA fly-rod record for 12-pound tippet.

Tony Accardo bought the company and moved its stock to Baton Rouge in 1981, where Accardo/Peck's Poppers Company continues to make top-quality cork poppers—the package that contained the popper in the photo states, "Ten coats of celluloid lacquers and epoxy sealers for that lustrous finish and durability." Tony's love of Peck's Poppers and that tradition is such that he is the creator and curator of the Peckinpaugh Historical Society. Available in some fly shops and mail order from Bass Pro Shops; Accardo/Peck's is wholesale only (see Sources, page 130).

Pobst's Keel Frog Popper
(Dick Pobst)

Hook: Mustad keel hook, size 4
Body: Cork, painted, yellow belly, green top with black and yellow spots
Legs: Green deer hair, tied in a bunch
Collar: Yellow hackle
Eyes: Painted, black on white
Notes: Designed for the keel hook—the fly stays hook-point-up on the retrieve. This is the frog; others are black with black legs and black with yellow bands. Available from Thornapple Orvis Shop (see Sources page 130).

Smith's Schnauzer
(Harry Smith)

Hook: Tiemco Stinger size 2
Tail: Black rabbit strip, fur down; pearl Krystal Flash; pearl Fly Flash
Body: White chenille
Back: Antelope ribbed with wire
Sides: Natural gray rabbit strips, fur out
Collar: Antelope stiffened with black silicone
Weedguard: Mason hard mono 25-pound, two strands
Notes: This is the surface-dapping, surface disturbing, in-the-bushes Harry Smith original, from Santa Ana, California. The name comes from when Harry was looking at the face of the fly, with its dark hood and fur squirting out to the side, it reminded him of the dog with that moniker.

An experimenter, Harry says, "I am doing a new—for me—technique. Decided to go completely hookless for the fun of it. My past yearly records for Oso Reservoir (Southern California) show that in an average three-hour morning bite, surface action, I average twenty to thirty strikes, land eight or ten bass.

"In November of 1996 I thought, what would happen if I didn't have any hook—if I didn't hurt the fish, would it come back right away and strike again? November is not exactly the best surface action but I gave it a try. On a Monday I had 157 strikes in three hours. I could not believe it. Went back the following Wednesday, 91 strikes. Friday was 137 hits.

"This past year, 1997, my best day was 225 surface takes in a three hour time span. The most hits by one fish—eight in less than a minute.

"No line, no reel, no guides, just the tip-top on the end of an old Silaflex 3-weight glass rod. The fly, ten marabou black blood feathers, two inches long, tightly wrapped on a hook shank with the curve and barb cut off. One inch of leader knotted to the tip-top and that's it. Last year I never lost a fly and three times the fish hit hard enough to pull my two-piece rod apart."

RAW's Flexo Popper
(Richard A. Whitner)

Hook: Mustad 9023SS, Tiemco 511S, Eagle Claw popper hook, Owner Cutting Point worm hook

Tail: Pearl Krystal Flash, White hen saddle tied on clipped off hook shank, attached to body with loop of mono

Underbody: Woody's plastic worm rattle; Fly Foam cut triangular; lead wire on rear of hook shank

Body: 1/4 inch Flexo tubing

Head: Flexo tubing is indented in front, making a forward-facing scoop

Eyes: Witchcraft adhesive prismatic

Gills: Red permanent marker

Notes: This fly is silver with a blue back made with permanent marker. Richard Whitner of New Orleans, Louisiana, says, "As an option, this fly can be tied without an inner body if the outer portion (the Flexo tubing)

is completely sealed with Loon's Soft Body Epoxy or Softex, trapping air inside. This fly has great action and should be played with for best results. When the fly is at a dead stop, the tail and rattle continue to give it action and sound." Available from Orvis (see Sources, page 130).

Spirit River's Foam-Tec Popper
(Spirit River)

Hook: Stinger, sizes 10 and 6

Tail: Hackle, Crystal Splash

Body: Pre-formed foam, painted

Legs: Round rubber

Collar: Hackle

Eyes: Solid plastic, black on yellow

Weedguard: Mason hard mono, double loops

Notes: This is the frog version; others are black, red, purple, yellow and a hot belly series with a fluorescent orange belly. Available wholesale from Spirit River.

Spirit River's Pro-Tec Popper
(Spirit River)

Hook: Stinger, sizes 10-2

Tail: Hackle, Crystal Splash

Body: Hard foam

Legs: Round rubber

Collar: Bucktail

Eyes: Doll, black on white

Weedguard: Mason hard mono

Notes: This is the frog version; others are black, pearl, chartreuse, yellow. Available wholesale from Spirit River.

Stewart's Dancing Frog
(Jim Stewart)

Hook: Stinger, size 2
Tail: White rubber strands
Body: Deer hair, white, gray, red
Head: Red deer hair
Eyes: Plastic, white with black pupil
Weedguard: Twin hard mono loops
Notes: Modeled after the famous Arbogast Hula Popper with its slanted face, fat-skinny-fat body, and rubber leg skirt. Besides red/white, also in frog colors of green/yellow.

Jim Stewart of Tampa, Florida, is quoted by Bob McNally in *Bassmaster* magazine, March 1992: "I learned that commercial streamers and bugs were limited in what they could do. I wanted some flies that could achieve the same things I could do with baitcasting lures. So I began to develop what I call plug flies."

McNally wrote: "A plug fly, as Stewart defines it, is a fly-rod bug that has built-in action. This is revolutionary in the fly-rod world because most streamers and poppers only have actions imparted to them by anglers. Plug flies, by design, dip and dive and wiggle and shake on retrieve—much like the old wooden plugs Stewart grew up casting in Tennessee."

Available from The Fly Shop and wholesale from Umpqua Feather Merchants. Jim Stewart ties for collectors (see Sources, page 130).

Sublett's Baby Bass
(Randy Sublett)

Hook: Mustad 3407, size 2/0
Tail: White marabou; pearl Flashabou
Body: Deer hair, white, green, black, in wedge shape
Eyes: Solid plastic, black on orange

Tullis Squirt Popper
(Larry Tullis)

Hook: Long-shank saltwater
Tail: Silver Flashabou; bucktail, tan, white
Body: White foam, painted silver on top
Gills: Red fabric paint
Eyes: Plastic, black on yellow
Notes: The innovative aspect of this popper is the hole drilled through its front, at a 45-degree angle, starting just above the hook eye and emerging above the eyes on its back. Larry Tullis, of Taylorsville, Utah says that with a long, hard pull on the fly line, this hollow tube in the foam causes water to squirt over the back of the popper and leaves a bubble trail. Available from Larry Tullis (see Sources, page 130).

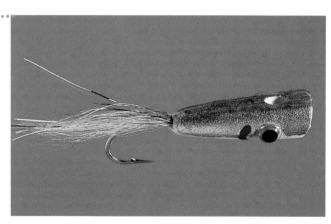

Walega's M.R. Foam Gerbubble Bug
(Michael R. Walega)

Hook: Mustad 37187 size 6
Tail: Yellow grizzly hackle tips, splayed
Collar: Yellow grizzly hackle
Body: Two layers Fly Foam, laminated; permanent
    marker, black spots
Side Hackle: Yellow grizzly hackle
Eyes: Doll eyes, black on yellow
Notes: Available through Michael R. Walega, M.R. Flies
(see Sources, page 130).

Walega's M.R. Frog
(Michael R. Walega)

Hook: Mustad 3366 size 2/0
Tail: Olive grizzly hackle tips, splayed; rubber legs,
    white, yellow, green, black
Body: Three layers Fly Foam, laminated; permanent
    marker, black spots
Legs: Rubber, white, yellow, green, black
Eyes: Doll eyes, black on yellow
Weedguard: Hard Mason 20-pound
Notes: Available through Michael R. Walega, M.R. Flies
(see Sources, page 130).

Walega's M.R. Minnow
(Michael R. Walega)

Hook: Mustad 32669CT size 1/0
Tail: Frayed-out large Flashabou Minnow Body, pearl
Underbody: Yellow Fly Foam
Body: Large Flashabou Minnow Body, pearl; green per-
    manent marker on back
Collar: Frayed-out large Flashabou Minnow Body, pearl
Head: Large Flashabou Minnow Body, pearl, hollowed
    out
Eyes: Doll eyes, black on yellow
Weight: Five turns .030 inch lead wire
Notes: Available through Michael R. Walega, M.R. Flies
(see Sources, page 130).

Whitlock's Deer Hair Bass Bug
(Dave Whitlock)

Hook: Stinger, sizes 2-10
Tail: Hackle, white, yellow, grizzly
Body: Deer hair, pale yellow, bright yellow, white
Legs: Pale yellow rubber
Collar: Yellow hackle
Eyes: Doll eyes, black on white
Weedguard: Mason hard mono 20-pound
Notes: This is the canary yellow version. Others include black/red; black/blue; black/yellow; black/peacock; frog; fruit cocktail; Porkey's Pet. Available from The Fly Shop and wholesale from Umpqua Feather Merchants.

Dave Whitlock of Midway, Arkansas, wrote in his book *L.L. Bean Fly Fishing For Bass Handbook*, 1988, "Bass will usually hold onto the soft-bodied bug several times longer than the hard body because these feel or taste more realistic to them. This is important if the bug is sitting still or moving slowly, because setting the hook takes more time than when you're using a taut line and a fast-moving bug. If your reaction is slow, soft bodies help a lot.

"Head and body designs vary according to what type of swimming action and noise is required to simulate the food creature.

"The Popper design has a blunt or cupped face that when twitched or jerked makes a splashy, popping, or gurgling disturbance; bass are strongly attracted to the sights and sounds of such flies. With some practice you can make a good bass popper talk to the fish. This talking would be sounds a struggling creature would make or those of another small fish splashing or feeding at the surface. These high-frequency sounds alert and direct bass to them. Poppers are a lot of fun to fish because of this action and the way bass break the surface to suck them down or come leaping violently on top of the popper."

Wyatt's Prismatic Yellow Popper
(Eddie Wyatt)

Hook: Tiemco 8089NP, size 10
Tail: Sixteen strands rainbow Krystal Flash over gray squirrel tail
Collar: Yellow Estaz
Body: 1/2 x 1/2-inch round yellow foam; silver prismatic lure tape
Eyes: Adhesive prismatic eyes, black on yellow
Gills: Red permanent marker
Notes: Before super gluing the foam to the hook, cover shank with thread, then cut bottom of body flat, then notch the bottom for the hook. When finished with fly, cover the foam body with Softex. Besides this yellow one, a silver one is available from Umpqua Feather Merchants (wholesale).

Denise Paul loves to catch bass on poppers at Barnes Butte Lake, Oregon.

Poppers

Carey Marcus with an eight-pound bass from Lake Fork, Texas.

Sliders

The pencil popper can be worked as a popper or a slider.

In his *Book of the Black Bass*, 1881, 1923, James Henshall wrote a description of some of the first sliders developed for bass, "The first bass bugs that I remember were made and sent to me by M.D. Butler of Indianapolis, Indiana, during the World's Fair at Chicago in 1893. They were made with plump, buoyant bodies, dressed with silk floss and feathers, and with long wings, hackles, tails, and streamers of prismatic hues."

Even though the popper is the most commonly used topwater fly for bass, don't overlook the slider. Because bass are often hooked on poppers, bass soon learn to avoid them, and the bigger bass become especially wary of poppers. In especially clear water, such as spring-fed Barnes Butte Lake in central Oregon, bass often demand the fly be swimming subsurface—they may track a surface fly, but won't take it until it slides underwater.

With its buoyant head of deer hair or foam, the slider merely slides along, sometimes slipping just under water, sometimes with a slight gurgling sound, swimming without fish-scaring noise, seducing bass with its quiet demeanor. When bass are in the shallows and it's windy, a slider often works better than a popper because the slider spends much of its time just under the surface, where the bass can see it. The popping noise of the popper is lost in the wind and wave disturbance.

With a wide head, some sliders can pop if worked briskly, and some sliders are wakers, generating a wave-pressure that bass feel with nerves in their lateral line and inner ear—a further evolutionary refinement that allows bass to track prey. Some of the most effective sliders incorporate a rabbit strip tail, which slithers along, pulsating with the retrieve, yet dangling when the fly is still. (The famous Dahlberg Diver with a rabbit-strip tail is covered in the chapter on divers. See Sources, page 130.)

The slider-style bass fly is deadly when fished as a subsurface fly via a sinking line because you can impart an up-and-down action by varying your retrieve. Also, bass zoom in on the underwater wave created by the slider head.

Barr's Little Brown Cat
(John Barr)

Hook: Tiemco 8089, size 6
Tail: Dark brown rabbit strip; gold Flashabou
Body: Red marabou
Collar: Dark brown marabou; dark brown deer hair
Head: Dark brown deer hair
Eyes: Doll eyes, black on yellow
Notes: John ties this fly to simulate the little brown catfish, prey for bass. A dentist living in Boulder, Colorado, John has access to a batch of private ponds and lakes where he field tests his designs. An intense fisherman, you can be confident that John's flies catch fish.

John says, "I was fishing at Rocky Mountain Arsenal and I caught this seven pound bass that had a little bull-

head catfish in his stomach, with part of it still in his throat. I thought, 'Hmmm, they must like these little bullheads.' This is a fun pattern, when it swims it pushes a little bow wake."

Burk's F.S. Floatin' Minnow
(Andy Burk)

Hook: Tiemco 300, size 2
Tail: White marabou, pearl Krystal Flash
Body: Dense white foam, epoxy, extra-fine pearlescent glitter
Head: Red permanent marker
Eyes: Adhesive, pearl with black pupil

Dahlberg's Dilg Slider
(Larry Dahlberg)

Hook: Stinger, size 2
Tail: Red Flashabou; grizzly hackle; fluorescent chartreuse rabbit strip
Collar: Fluorescent chartreuse deer hair
Head: Fluorescent chartreuse deer hair
Eyes: Doll eyes, black on yellow
Weedguard: Mason hard mono 20-pound
Notes: This is the chartreuse rendition of Dahlberg's version of the Dilg Slider, named after Will Dilg, one of the first to apply hair, feathers and cork to the hook to catch bass in the early 1900s. Other colors include

black; white. Available wholesale from Umpqua Feather Merchants.

Dahlberg's Mega Slop Slider
(Larry Dahlberg)

Hook: Tiemco 811S, size 1/0
Tail: Purple Flashabou; red marabou; Big Fly Fiber, black
Collar: Deer hair, red, black
Head: Black deer hair
Eyes: Doll eyes, black on yellow
Weedguard: Wire loop
Notes: Dahlberg designed this fly to ease through heavy cover, teasing bass to strike.

Dahlberg's Skipper
(Larry Dahlberg)

Hook: Tiemco 811S, size 1/0
Tail: Pearl Krystal Flash; silver Flashabou; badger hackle
Fins: Hen hackle
Collar: Deer hair, white
Head: White deer hair
Eyes: Doll eyes, black on yellow
Weedguard: Mason hard mono 20-pound
Notes: This is the minnow version, designed for a fast retrieve, skipping the bug across the water. Frog version available wholesale from Umpqua Feather Merchants.

Dave's Bend Back Muddler
(Dave Rabe)

Hook: Stinger, bent, size 1/0
Tail: Marabou; grizzly hackle; rubber strands; Krystal Flash; all purple
Collar: Purple deer hair
Head: Purple deer hair
Eyes: Solid plastic, black on yellow
Notes: This is the purple version. Dave has eight others that he ties.

Dave's Marabou Waker
(Dave Rabe)

Hook: Kink shank popper, size 1/0
Tail: Green marabou over chartreuse marabou; chartreuse Krystal Flash
Body: Chartreuse foam
Legs: Chartreuse rubber strands
Eyes: Doll eyes
Notes: Dave says, "This bait in various colors provides a large, bulky silhouette with a great deal of action. The design allows a quiet presentation but moves a lot of water."

Dave's Zonker Streamer
(Dave Rabe)

Hook: Extra-long shank streamer, sizes 4 to 2/0
Tail: Rabbit Zonker strip, olive
Body: Palmered Zonker strip, olive
Collar: Deer hair, olive
Head: Deer hair, olive
Eyes: Solid plastic, black on yellow
Notes: Dave says, "This fly works well on top as an injured baitfish, but really excels as an after-dark streamer on a sink-tip line, when you need to push a lot of water."

Earhart's Ultimate Slider
(Vann Earhart)

Hook: Mustad saltwater hook, size 1
Tail: White hackle tips, blue marabou, blue Krystal Flash, blue Flashabou
Body: Foam; white with blue back, gray scale, red belly spot
Collar: White hackle
Eyes: Painted, black on white on black
Notes: A gorgeous example of the modern hard-foam slider, this is just one of dozens of versions. Available wholesale from Ultimate Poppers (see Sources, page 130).

EdgeWater's Spinster
(EdgeWater)

Hook: Saltwater or Stinger, sizes 2-3/0
Tail: Hackle, Krystal Flash, bucktail, marabou
Collar: Marabou
Body: Foam
Eyes: Solid eyes, black on yellow; lead eyes available
Weedguard: Plastic-covered wire loops
Notes: This is the yellow version. Others are white, purple, black, chartreuse, blue. Available from EdgeWater (see Sources, page 130).

EdgeWater's Spook-A-Like
(EdgeWater)

Hook: Saltwater long shank, sizes 1/0 and 2/0
Tail: Marabou, Krystal Flash
Body: Foam; epoxy over paint, lead weight
Eyes: Solid eyes, black on yellow
Notes: This is the yellow version; others are white, purple, black, chartreuse, blue and peppermint. EdgeWater's catalog states: "This fly has a side-to-side, darting, walk-the-dog action, which is a proven fish catcher. We believe it's as much fun to fish with as any fly we've created." The names derives from Zara Spook, a traditional, deadly lure for bass. Available finished or as a kit from EdgeWater (see Sources, page 130).

Ellis Grinnel Fly
(Jack Ellis)

Hook: Mustad 3366, sizes 2/0, 2, 6
Thread: 3/0 monocord, black
Tail: Thin, natural brown rabbit strip, 4 inches long
Body: Natural deer-body hair
Collar: Natural deer-body hair tips
Head: Spun deer hair
Eyes: 4mm doll eyes
Weedguard: .019 hard mono
Notes: Jack Ellis of Woodville, Texas is author of *Bassin' With a Fly Rod*, 1994, where he says, "This is, without a doubt, the most effective fly in my arsenal. I tie it in three colors. Natural works best but black and olive followed closely behind, especially on cloudy days.

"Either hollow or solid eyes can be used, depending on the amount of buoyancy desired. The eyes of a water snake are very inconspicuous, but I use them on this fly to regulate buoyancy. Neutral buoyancy can easily be achieved by trimming and by the type of eyes selected. The fly should be slightly buoyant so it will ride low in the surface film when fished topwater, and it should be tied with neutral buoyancy when fished near the bottom on a sinking line. I tie this fly in various colors, but the above pattern is by far the most productive in my waters. This fly looks so realistic slithering through the weeds, you'll have to resist the urge to eat it yourself."

Gaines's Sneaky Pete
(Gaines/Phillips)

Hook: Mustad bass popper, size 2
Tail: Synthetic material, chartreuse
Body: Cork, chartreuse
Legs: White rubber
Collar: Black hackle
Eyes: Painted, black on white on black
Notes: A fine example of the traditional cork slider. This is the Sneaky Pete version; there are dozens of others. Gaines/Phillips still makes their poppers and sliders

from cork although quality cork is difficult to obtain. Available from Cortland and wholesale (see Sources, page 130).

In his *Book of the Black Bass*, 1881, 1923, James Henshall included a color plate with three Wilder Feather Minnows. He quoted an article written in 1921 by B.F. Wilder:

> "I hit upon a head made of cork and a body composed of long, springy cock hackles. These feathers were tied in on either side of the hook-shank with the natural curve of the feathers of one side opposed to the curve of those forming the other side, which resulted in a very flexible body with the appearance of substance and of almost no weight. When the completed lure floated in its testing vessel it floated barely awash; it appeared to struggle helplessly at the slightest movement of the leader."

Although constructed with the cone-shaped head we would now call a slider, the Feather Minnows were grouped under the general term of bugs.

Galloway's Foamin' Perch
(Bill Galloway)

Hook: Standard long shank, size 1/0
Body: Yellow foam
Wing: Marabou, yellow, olive; copper Krystal Flash; yellow grizzly hackle
Gills: Red hackle
Eyes: Solid plastic, black on yellow
Weedguard: Mason hard mono 20-pound
Notes: This is the perch version. Others include shad, golden shiner, silver shiner, black, frog.

Gammel's Weed Runner Yellow Slider
(Bill Gammel)

Hook: Stinger, size 1/0
Tail: Yellow marabou
Body: Yellow chenille palmered with yellow hackle
Legs: Round rubber, white
Wing: White closed-cell foam
Head: White closed-cell foam
Weedguard: Notch in the foam wing
Notes: This is the yellow version. Others are frog, black, purple, white, chartreuse. For years Bill Gammel of Highlands, Texas successfully fished a keel-style marabou streamer, but he always thought a floating version would be ideal. Gammel investigated foam, but he says, "I couldn't figure out how to make the foam work. I struggled with it for six months, enjoying none of it.

When Gammel discovered a soft-plastic jerkbait indented with a groove along its back for the hook (a Sluggo), he knew he had the solution for his fly. He says, "I cut a hole in the back of the foam wing, then a little groove in the top of the wing that allows the hook point to settle down into the foam, so the hook isn't exposed."

Gammel describes his Weedrunner series as "basically a Woolly Bugger with a foam wing." The foam wing/weed guard keeps the hook inverted; the body and tail swim underwater, providing bulk and a broad silhouette to provoke strikes. The Weedrunner Slider features a bullet-head style of chenille and foam; the built-up head and rubber legs push water, as well as adding color and motion, all of which cause bass to strike. (See Gammel's Weedrunner Popper, page 130.)

Helm's Deer Hair Mouse
(Chris Helm)

Hook: Partridge GRS S4 (John Holden Heavyweight Sea Hook) sizes 2 to 6/0; Daiichi 2720 Stinger, sizes 1 to 5/0

Weight: Optional, lead wire on hook at rear for balance, covered with thread and epoxy

Thread: Dynacord or UNI-Cord 3/0; Gudebrod G

Tail: Ultra Suede, gray, black, brown or pink

Body: Stacked whitetail deer body or rump hair

Ears: Same as tail

Whiskers: Moose hair

Eyes: Black plastic bead

Weedguard: Mason hard mono 20-pound

Notes: Chris Helm of Toledo, Ohio is the star of the video "Spinning Deer Hair" in the series Hooked On Fly

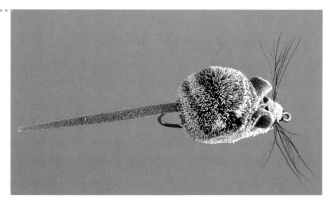

Tying, Bennett/Watt Productions. His newest video is "Tying Hair Bugs With Chris Helm." He is also Whitetail Fly Tying Supplies (see Sources). The tradition of tying Deer Hair Mice for bass dates back to the 1920s when Orley Tuttle developed his Tuttle's Mouse. A catalog advertisement from 1926 shows the fly complete with eyes, ears and tail.

Jensen's Floating Smelt
(Milt Jensen)

Hook: Tiemco 300, sizes 2 and 6

Tail: Medium gray marabou

Underbody: 2mm Fly Body foam, top shaded with light gray permanent marker

Body: Medium pearl Minnow Body Mylar tubing

Gills: Red permanent marker, optional

Eyes: Yellow acrylic with black pupil; body covered with Sally Hansen's Hard As Nails

Notes: This is the smelt version. Others are Golden Shiner, Glass Minnow, Fire Tiger, Blue Back, Perch; some feature stainless-steel hooks, larger sizes, flexible epoxy coatings and wire weedguards. Floating Smelt available from Umpqua Feather Merchants (wholesale).

Milt's Minnows available through The Fly Shop and from Milt Jensen, a guide from Chico, California (see Sources, page 130).

McMillan's McFrog
(Dave McMillan)

Hook: Stainless steel, 3/0

Tail: Olive, brown grizzly saddle hackle

Body: Deer hair, olive, yellow, dark brown

Collar: Olive, brown grizzly hackle

Eyes: Large solid plastic, black on yellow

Weedguard: Cortland black mono 50-pound

Notes: Dave McMillan of Fort Worth, Texas has developed a whole system of hunting 5-pound-plus bass by presenting floating flies subsurface, using his own system of heads and integrated running lines, as shown in his video "Combat Fly Fishing" (see Sources, page 130). Fly available from Umpqua Feather Merchants (wholesale).

McMillan's McMurderer
(Dave McMillan)

Hook: Stainless steel, 4/0
Tail: Rust brown rabbit strip
Body: Rust brown deer hair
Collar: Rust brown hackle
Eyes: Large solid plastic, black on orange
Weedguard: Cortland black mono 50-pound
Notes: Available from Umpqua Feather Merchants (wholesale).

McMillan's McSnake
(Dave McMillan)

Hook: Stainless steel, 3/0
Tail: Dark brown grizzly saddle hackle
Body: Deer hair, dark olive, dark brown
Collar: Brown hackle
Eyes: Large solid plastic, black on yellow
Weedguard: Cortland black mono 50-pound
Notes: Available from Umpqua Feather Merchants (wholesale).

Mercer's Lemming
(Mike Mercer)

Hook: Tiemco Stinger, 8089NP, size 2
Tail: Black round rubber, knotted
Body: Deer hair
Underbody: Australian opossum on hide
Legs: Black round rubber, knotted
Head: Foam, brown
Eyes: Solid plastic, black on amber

Notes: In his 1925 book, *The Fly Rod for Bass*, Cal Johnson wrote, "Bugging for bass has become a very popular method of fly rod angling and great sport can be derived from using them. The bass leaps upward as he strikes the bass-bug and a far more spectacular battle results than when he strikes under water. When fishing the shallows and along the shoreline, late in the afternoon or evening, the floating bass-bug will prove a delightful means of bringing bass to the net."

Although not labeled as such, one of the illustrations in that chapter is of a Tuttle's Mouse. Rodent imitations were part of the early bass-bug scene and still capture our imaginations as well as catching bass.

Mike Mercer of Redding, California, has crafted a clever combination of traditional deer hair with modern foam and epoxy, round rubber legs, Australian opossum fur and realistic eyes. Available from The Fly Shop and wholesale from Umpqua Feather Merchants.

Messinger's Frog
(Joe Messinger)

Hook: Stinger, sizes 6-10
Body: Deer hair, white, chartreuse, black
Legs: Bucktail, black, olive
Eyes: Plastic, black on white
Weedguard: Mason hard mono 20-pound
Notes: All fly fishermen that cast flies for bass are convinced that bass eat frogs, whether frogs are in evidence or not. And although frogs inhabit most bass waters, bass eat frog flies whether frogs are in evidence or not.

The Messinger Frog is a traditional bass bug, included in a color plate in John Alden Knight's book *Black Bass*, 1949. In his book *Black Bass Fishing*, 1952, Robert Page Lincoln states, "A fine angler by the name of Joseph Messinger of Morgantown, West Virginia put out

the first buckhair frog, and it is possible it is one of the most successful in the field".

Living in the same town as his father before him, Joe Messinger, Jr. continues the tradition by tying the Messinger Frog at angling shows. Available wholesale from Umpqua Feather Merchants.

Muddler Minnow
(Don Gapen)

Hook: Streamer, various sizes
Tail: Mottled turkey feather
Body: Gold tinsel
Wing: White calf or gray squirrel; mottled turkey feather
Collar: Deer hair tips
Head: Spun and clipped deer hair
Notes: This particular specimen was tied by Jack Ellis, author of *Bassin' with a Fly Rod*, who, like many others, has modified the original. Here he substitutes red fox squirrel in the wing and adds strands of gold Krystal Flash. However, the standard dressing is not his first choice. In his book he says, "Every fly fisher has a special fly they know will do the job when all else fails. Mine is the Marabou Muddler. This is the design I use for all of my standard streamers, varying the color accordingly. I have seen this fly tied with a huge deer-hair head and a lot of fluffy dressing that makes it float on top of the water like a bug. This is not the version. My idea of a Marabou Muddler is that presented by Terry Hellekson, in his book *Popular Fly Patterns*. When properly tied, these flies neither sink nor float; they are neutrally buoyant. Depth, if desired, is achieved with a sinking line, leader or split shot, not by tying lead into the fly which spoils its action. With a number of colors in sizes 6 to 10, I can effectively represent all of the fifty-plus species of baitfish that occur in my part of the Lone Star state."

Popular variations for the Marabou Muddler include: deleting the mottled turkey, which is hard to find, expensive, and shreds after the first cast; crimson red hackle, short, for the tail; varied tinsel for the body; a wing topping of peacock herl over a wing of marabou and either gray or red fox squirrel or calf tail. Color schemes are black, brown, gray, olive, yellow and white.

In his book, *The Practical Fly Fisherman*, 1953, 1975, A.J. McClane wrote: "Prima donna of the smallmouth flies, and I say this with no reservation, is the sparse Muddler Minnow. In August of 1949, I wrote an article for *Field & Stream* called "Bass Flies, Old and New." Among the new ones was a pattern known as the Muddler Minnow, a fly tied by Don Gapen in Nipigon, Ontario. Don's intention was an imitation of the darter minnow, a streamer for big trout. It proved to be excellent for big squaretails. According to my notes, the Muddler accounted for more than twenty brook trout of over four pounds during the time I used it. However, I used this streamer as a dry fly.

"Guy Kibbee and I were fishing a small Quebec pond the first time I tested the Muddler. A few large trout were breaking in close to shore, and we took turns working them over—five minutes at the paddle and five with the rod. Neither of us seemed to have what the fish wanted, and then I remembered Don's new fly. My next cast put the slim brown Muddler beyond a rising trout, and I jerked the line to make it sink. The fly went down, then bobbed up again. I pulled the line harder, but the deer hair hackle kept popping back up. On the sixth or seventh pull a five and a half pound brook trout sucked the fly under. But this was only the beginning. We took more than ten trout that day, and none was less than four pounds, and one that weighed over six pounds. I should qualify this by saying that this particular lake holds plenty of squaretails weighing over four pounds, but they are very temperamental surface feeders. In any event, Guy and I were convinced that Don had inadvertently created a terrific trout dry fly.

"There was something about the Muddler, though, that smacked of smallmouth, and that was the reason why this pattern was introduced in an article on bass flies. We weren't disappointed. Right after I came back from Quebec, I went to work on a number of heavily fished bass waters, and in the light of my fishing since that time, I would rate this pattern as a most reliable smallmouth fly. Action usually makes the difference."

McClane's description of his deadly strip-pause retrieve that sinks a buoyant-head fly comes as no surprise to the well-informed largemouth or smallmouth fishermen of the 21st century. But he also describes working his way downstream on the West Branch of the Delaware River for smallmouth with a two-fly cast, with "a size 6 Muddler at the point and a size 10 on the dropper—the heavier fly on the point helps straighten the cast out. Syd Field started at the lower end of the run with an identical two-fly cast. He worked his flies upstream, using a natural drift, imparting no motion to his flies. I started at the head of the run, casting downstream, and skidding the flies back. At the end of the first round, seven nice smallmouths had gobbled the downstream casts, and only one came to Syd's drift. I waded back upstream using the drift, and this time Syd worked his two flies downstream. He took five bass and I caught a chub.

"We actually did this over and over again in various parts of the river, and the downstream man always nailed more and larger bass. Simply get enough line out to cover that place that looks like a possibility and let the fly bounce back over the surface, holding your rod high and retrieving rather slowly."

A final note of interest on the Muddler. In his book *The Essential Fly Tier*, 1976, J. Edson Leonard wrote, "The Muddler received its name in a curious way. By dictionary definition, the word Muddler can mean a stirring stick, a person who muddles through his day, or a miller's thumb—any of several, small freshwater sculpins of the genus Cottus, whose heads are thumb-like. Don Gapen, the reputed creator of the Muddler as a superfly for brook trout, patterned it after the sculpin. But, depending on its size and the way it is fished, the Muddler can be much more than a sculpin; it can be a grasshopper, a stonefly, a caddis, any minnow, or just about anything short of a mayfly spinner or a midge, at the election of the user.

"Patterns are far from standard. Basically, the Muddler is a feather-hair streamer with a clipped deer-hair head. The body often is tinsel. The tail is speckled turkey and the wings are mixtures of hair (calf tail or squirrel) and speckled turkey. The clipped-hair head finishes the fly. Years ago, before the Muddler was so named, it was called ball head. There was a slight difference—the ball head had hackle streamers instead of turkey-quill fibers."

This brief history of the Muddler illustrates a fact of life about fly patterns—similar patterns or recipes are often developed or invented during a similar time frame in different parts of the country. A true breakthrough in fly design is no less valid if two individual tiers come up with the same idea, but solving the puzzle as to who originally invented a specific fly or design can get tricky. Often, the only way we have of establishing a date of conception is by the written record, but that means an inventor must come to the attention of a writer, and an accurate writer, as well. Unfortunately, the exact origins of many of our favorite flies and their designs are simply lost to time. However, in spite of that we can enjoy a pleasing fly; some of us prefer to present it to fish, while others simply enjoy tying flies. After all, fly fishing and tying is supposed to be fun.

Nelson's Bunny Ribbit
(Carter Nelson)

Hook: Mustad 3366, size 1

Legs: Mason hard mono, 20-pound punched through rabbit strips, olive

Body: Wool, white or yellow for belly, green, olive or brown for the back; optional, lead wire for deeper sinking

Eyes: Doll eyes, black on white

Notes: This is the all-wool version. In *Fly Tyer* magazine, Winter 1996, Carter Nelson of Lawrenceville, Georgia wrote about his fly: "From my years of fishing and guiding for largemouths, I knew that a feeding bass responds to several stimuli: movement, shape, color, size and smell. A good bass pattern should imitate these characteristics as found in natural frogs, with the exception of smell, though I suppose you could add an artificial scent (eau de toad, perhaps?).

"Then I turned my attention to frogs. I caught a mess of them, which wasn't exactly easy, and took notes on their appearance in the water. When I released or tried to recapture them, the critter didn't skitter, jump or pop on the surface; they put their strong legs to work. The frogs dove deep and swam with frantic kicks—the same as if they were being chased by a bass or other

predator. I decided the most important aspect of a frog pattern should be the imitation of this kicking action.

"The Bunny Ribbit is named for the Zonker-strip legs, which I think more closely match the real thing than hair or feather legs. On my early models the rabbit strips fouled around the hook. I solved the problem by tying hard-monofilament supports to the hook, piercing holes in the Zonker strips, and threading the mono through the rabbit strips. This keeps the legs splayed and adds a realistic kicking action as the frog is retrieved.

"I use wool for the body because it soaks up water and makes the bug sink, it can be trimmed to shape, and it comes in froggy colors (green, olive, brown for the back; yellow and white for the belly)."

Nelson's Chili Ribbit
(Carter Nelson)

Hook: Mustad 3366, size 1; or long shank as shown, bent upwards by the head (frog with just its eyes above water)

Legs: Mason hard mono, 20-pound punched through rabbit strips, olive

Body: Wool belly, white or yellow; for back and front, green, olive or brown deer hair

Eyes: Solid eyes, black on yellow

Notes: In the same article in *Fly Tyer* magazine, Winter 1996, Carter wrote: "Next, I wanted to design a frog pattern that I could fish over structure, that would float in the surface film. A deer-hair body worked okay, but the bug sometimes swam upside down or spun in the water. To counter this, I used a technique that David

"Chili" Childers and I had been experimenting with—stacking deer hair over wool.

"The wool belly absorbs water and acts as ballast to keep the frog from turning over or spinning, while the buoyant deer-hair back keeps the frog afloat."

Nix's Shineabou Shiner
(Jimmy Nix)

Hook: Tiemco 811S, size 4 and 1/0
Tail: White bucktail; dun hackle; Krystal Flash, silver, peacock
Body: Gray Antron
Gills: Red marabou
Collar: Deer hair, natural or gray
Head: Deer hair, natural or gray
Eyes: Plastic, black on white
Weedguard: 20-pound hard Mason
Notes: Other versions include the Woolhead Shineabou Shiner, the Fuzzabou Shad and the closely related deer-

hair and wool versions of the Shineabou Shad. Available wholesale from Umpqua Feather Merchants.

Ryan's Disc Frog
(Thomas C. Ryan, Jr.)

Hook: TMC 8089 Stinger, size 2
Tail: Rubber strands, green, yellow
Body: Deer hair spun and cut to disc shape; yellow with green bands on top, yellow with hot pink bands on bottom
Eyes: Doll or solid plastic eyes
Notes: The key to this design is the flattened disc shape, like a "flying saucer" UFO, with the hook coming out of a flat side. Tom Ryan of says, "The Disc Frog has great side-to-side action when fished with a loop knot such as a Duncan loop, but is a bitch to cast."

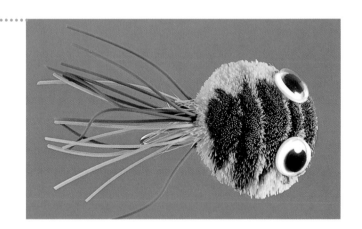

Ryan's Hell-Cat
(Thomas C. Ryan, Jr.)

Hook: Stinger, size 2; rear, straight-eye, extra-long shank, size 6 with bend and point clipped off
Tail: Purple hackle; pearl Flashabou
Body: Rear, palmered purple hackle; hinge, two loops of mono; front, spun and clipped deer hair, orange, brown
Eyes: Doll or solid plastic eyes
Weight: Lead wire wrapped around hook bend, with top end of wire extending down from body; super glue
Weedguard: Mason hard mono 20-pound, double loops
Notes: The snout on the body is pointed and rounded; the top has a blunt edge in front of the eyes, then the

middle of the top, rear half, is shaved, leaving just a fringe on top above the eyes. Tom calls it "a jointed surface fly with a funny haircut".

Ryan's Injured Sunfish
(Thomas C. Ryan, Jr.)

Hook: TMC Stinger 8089, size 6
Tail: Olive deer hair stiffened with silicone
Body: Deer hair, olive, light olive, orange, blue
Fins: Deer hair, olive, light olive, stiffened with silicone
Eyes: Solid plastic, black on orange
Weedguard: Mason hard mono 20-pound, double loops
Notes: Tom sometimes substitutes marabou for the tail. The hook comes out of the side of the sunfish body, so the fly lays flat on the water.

Spirit River's Foam-Tec Slider
(Spirit River)

Hook: Stinger, sizes 10 and 6
Tail: Marabou, Crystal Splash
Body: Pre-formed foam
Legs: Round rubber
Collar: Hackle
Eyes: Solid plastic, black on yellow
Weedguard: Mason hard mono
Notes: This is the purple version; others are a diver in black and red. Available wholesale from Spirit River.

Spirit River's Pro-Tec Slider
(Spirit River)

Hook: Stinger, sizes 10 and 6
Tail: Hackle, Crystal Splash
Body: Hard foam
Legs: Round rubber
Collar: Bucktail
Eyes: Doll, black on white
Weedguard: Mason hard mono
Notes: This is the black version; others are frog, pearl, chartreuse, yellow. Available wholesale from Spirit River.

Sublett's Sneaky Snake
(Randy Sublett)

Hook: Mustad 3407, size 2/0
Tail: Brown rabbit strip; copper Krystal Flash
Body: Deer hair, white, brown
Eyes: Solid plastic, black on orange

Two-Legged Frog
(tied by Walt Benscoter)

Hook: Mustad 3366, size 2
Body: Natural deer hair
Legs: Red fox squirrel tail
Notes: Walt Benscoter of Rochester, Minnesota says, "This is a classic pattern no longer found in the marketplace. I used this fly as early as 1943 and it was present in my father's tackle box well before that time. This pattern remains a favorite of mine for stream or river smallmouth throughout the hot part of the summer."

Verduin's Jointed Hair Ball Bug
(Mike Verduin)

Hook: Stinger, sizes 2-10
Tail: Jointed, olive grizzly hackle
Tail Collar: Olive grizzly hackle
Body: Deer hair, white, olive, yellow, black
Eyes: Solid plastic eyes, black on amber
Weedguard: Mason hard mono 20-pound
Notes: This is the frog version from Mike Verduin of Irving, Texas. Others include black; natural.

Whitlock's Flashabou Floating Muddler
(Dave Whitlock)

Hook: Tiemco 300, size 4
Tag: Red tying thread
Body: Gold Mylar tubing
Wing: Orange marabou; gold, pearl Flashabou; peacock herl
Collar: Deer hair, golden brown, black
Head: Golden brown deer hair
Eyes: Doll eyes, black on yellow
Weedguard: Mason hard mono 20-pound
Notes: This is the gold version; others are black; silver. Available from Umpqua Feather Merchants (wholesale). In his book *L.L. Bean Fly Fishing for Bass Handbook*, 1988, Dave Whitlock, of Midway, Arkansas wrote, "Muddler

Minnow—one of the most versatile and effective bass flies. It can be dressed to float, dive, or swim, and looks like many bass foods."

Whitlock's Hare Waterpup
(Dave Whitlock)

Hook: Tiemco 7999, size 2
Tail: Rabbit strip
Body: Purple Antron
Rib: Copper wire
Wing: Continuation of tail, Matuka style
Collar: Deer hair
Head: Deer hair
Eyes: Doll eye, black on red
Weedguard: Mason hard mono 20-pound
Notes: This is the purple version; others are olive, black. Available from Umpqua Feather Merchants (wholesale).

Whitlock's Mouserat
(Dave Whitlock)

Hook: Stinger, size 6
Tail: Brown leather
Body: Deer hair
Ears: Brown leather
Whiskers: Black moose
Head: Deer hair
Eyes: Permanent marker, black
Weedguard: Mason hard mono 20-pound
Notes: This is the natural version; also available in black from The Fly Shop and wholesale from Umpqua Feather Merchants.

Whitlock's Wigglelegs Frog
(Dave Whitlock)

Hook: Stinger, sizes 2 and 6
Legs: Bucktail, white, chartreuse; green grizzly hackle
Body: Deer hair, white, chartreuse, green, black
Arms: Rubber, black, fluorescent yellow, white, chartreuse or all white, knotted
Eyes: Doll eyes, black on yellow
Weedguard: Mason hard mono 20-pound
Notes: Dave Whitlock wrote about this fly in *The Fly-Tyer's Almanac*, Boyle and Whitlock, 1975. Available wholesale from Umpqua Feather Merchants.

Yamagata's Extended Body Mouse
(Jeff Yamagata)

Hook: TMC 8089, sizes 2-10
Tail: Brown vernille
Body: Rainey's Float Foam; rabbit strips or muskrat
Legs: Brown vernille
Collar: Deer hair
Head: Deer hair
Ears: Brown chamois
Eyes: Solid plastic, black on white
Whiskers: Brown Ocean Hair
Notes: Available at A-1 Fish Fly Fishing Supplies (see Sources, page 130).

Yamagata's Floating Shad
(Jeff Yamagata)

Hook: Tiemco 511S, sizes 6-2/0
Tail: White marabou
Body: Foam; Mylar tubing; epoxy
Eyes: Doll eyes or adhesive
Notes: Available at A-1 Fish Fly Fishing Supplies (see Sources, page 130).

Yamagata's Water Snake
(Jeff Yamagata)

Hook: TMC 8089, sizes 2-10
Tail: Ultra chenille twisted, olive, yellow
Body: Spun McFlyfoam, yellow, olive
Eyes: Solid plastic, black on amber
Tongue: Silicone strands, black with red tip
Notes: Available at A-1 Fish Fly Fishing Supplies (see Sources, page 130).

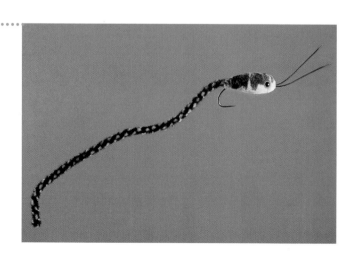

When the wind kicks up and bass are in shallow water, a slider will often be more effective than a popper because the slider glides under water, under the waves, triggering a strike.

Sliders

Fishing an Oregon pond with his favorite black nymph, Jon Hazen doesn't let cold water stop him. The author has taken bass just under the surface on deer-hair floating divers in 56-degree water but with repeated presentations to the same spot.

Floating Divers

Floating divers are incredibly effective when bass are in shallow water. When bass are deeper, floating divers are deadly when fished on a sinking-line-and-leader setup that probes the depth where the bass are foraging.

Some of the deadliest flies for bass are floaters that dive on the retrieve. The sudden diving of fleeing prey—the fly—usually triggers the strike, but this tactic is further enhanced because the fly pushes water as it dives, which bass detect as fleeing prey.

When you intersperse a pause in the retrieve, the floating diver tries to gain the surface, imparting an up-and-motion, simulating prey that is either naturally swimming or prey that is struggling, depending on your retrieve. Impart a swift retrieve, causing the diver to descend steeply, or less so, depending on the effect you want. You can use a floating or sink-tip line for shallow-holding bass, or full-sink line for bass lower in the water column. Vary the leader length to fine-tune your presentation to get that fly right in the bass's face. Floating divers are deadly.

Betts Bull-it Head
(John Betts)

Hook: Mustad 33903, size 1/0
Tail: Grizzly hackle; yellow marabou
Weight: .025 lead wire
Body: Closed-cell foam (Evasote), white; permanent
    marker, olive, black
Diving Lip: Clear .010 Mylar
Eyes: Dressmaker pins, black head
Notes: The frog version in size 1/0 and the black in size 2
available from The Fly Shop and wholesale from
Umpqua Feather Merchants.

John Betts of Denver, Colorado named his fly Bull-it
Head because he originally wanted to imitate baby bullhead. Black mimics the bullhead and bullfrog tadpoles.
He said, "The biggest bass I've taken was eight and a
half pounds, and she was the hardest bass I've ever
taken. It was here in Colorado.

"That big female came in within seven feet of me
and just sat in some reeds. I kept casting with just the
leader off the tip of the rod, and I kept casting past
where she had her head and the front half of her body
sticking out. I could tell by the position of her fins how
she regarded the action of the fly going by.

"If it was too fast, her fins would kind of fold up, and
she'd sink down a little bit in the water, maybe an inch or
so. If the fly went too slow, her eyes would be looking at
all kinds of different things. Finally, after 40 or 50 casts, I
found that I could keep her attention at certain speeds,
so I slowed it down on one cast, then a little bit faster on
subsequent casts, and she came up and took it."

John favors retrieving parallel to cover. His favorite
retrieve: "I let it sit out there, until the ripples get about
two or three feet away. Then I give it just enough

twitch, just a slight pull, to move it about a quarter of an
inch, just enough to turn it on its axis, to pivot. I don't
want it to move forward. And let it sit again. I'm always
amazed at how many fish are sitting under it. You turn it
too much and it will flush them.

"Then I start giving it 18-inch pulls—just enough to
get it to go under and just enough to get it to wiggle.
You don't want it zooming through the water—the
longer it's in the water, the more chance you've got. I
tune each fly to fish slowly so you can keep it in the
fishing area for as long as possible.

"An angler I sold a Bull-it Head to in Iowa sent me a
picture of a smallmouth he caught with it that was 29
inches long."

Author's note: since I am a catch-and-recatch fisherman, I disliked the large bump of steel remaining when
you bend down the barb, and when compared to more
modern, chemically-sharpened hooks, the hook-point
area is too large in diameter. Using a Dremel Tool, I
ground away the excess metal, then with a hook hone I
gained a sharp point, which increased my hook-up rate
considerably. I use the same technique on another popular bass hook that has no counterpart in modern, chemically-sharpened hooks, the Mustad 3366.

Dahlberg's Diving Bug
(Larry Dahlberg)

Hook: Stinger, size 2
Tail: Light blue marabou; peacock herl; gold Flashabou;
    grizzly hackle, blue, purple
Collar: Deer hair, purple, blue, black
Head: Purple deer hair
Weedguard: Mason hard mono 20-pound
Notes: This is the purple/blue version. Other colors
include black/grizzly; brown/grizzly; yellow/grizzly; bum-
ble bee; frog. Available wholesale from Umpqua Feather
Merchants.

Larry Dahlberg of Taylors Falls, Minnesota told me
he first developed his diver in 1977 when he was 18 years

old. He says, "I had a particular fish I was trying to
catch, a big bass, and I wanted to catch it on a fly rod. It
was in the spring and the bass would follow poppers all
the time. I wanted to get something that would dive

under the water and swim back up. I changed the shape of the deer hair to make the fly do what it needed to do."

That bass weighed 6 pounds 7 ounces; the Dahlberg Diver has since tricked boxcar loads of bass and other predator species, as well as spawning countless variations of the original Dahlberg Diver design. And although originally conceived for largemouth, this diver is deadly on smallmouth and all other predator fish as well.

"What's most important to understand," Larry says, "is that a diver wants to go deeper than the fly line is. You've got a floating fly line, you've got a leader attached, you pull the diver, the diver's gonna go deeper than the fly line.

"Therefore, if we use a sink-tip or full-sinking fly line, which I use a lot, and I let the line lay on the bottom, and I strip the fly in, the fly's gonna grind the bottom and make contact, just like a crankbait would.

"Here's the most effective way I know to fish a diver. If I wanted to turn them in, I would have at least twelve to fifteen world records that I've caught using this technique, with a full-sinking line, a long leader and a diver. You have to visualize this: the water is eight feet deep, I have a nine-foot leader, a full-sinking line, a diver that's dressed so it floats. I cast to a weed wall that's rooted in eight feet of water, I let the fly line sink to the bottom. But because the leader is a foot longer than the water is deep, the fly is still on the surface. I give it one quick strip, bloop, it goes down at a real steep angle, then it'll float right back to the surface. If I want to, I can go strip, strip, strip, strip, and the diver will continue to go all the way to the bottom, until it impacts the bottom and I'll feel it. If I stop, the diver will tilt it's head up and swim all the way back to the surface. And I can pop it again if I want to.

"I'm fishing the water both horizontally and vertically, and I'm creating some powerful strike triggers. One, the fly actually touching the bottom; two, the fly diving down; three, the fly swimming back up; and four, the popping noise. Those are four of the most powerful triggers there are, no matter where you fish.

"Doing this, I've caught muskies over thirty pounds, pike over thirty pounds, an eighteen-pound tiger fish on the Zambezi River when the world record at that time was seven pounds on a fly. In Tierra Del Fuego, in five consecutive casts, I hooked browns over twenty pounds, after having pounded the hole using all the traditional flies and doing what the Argentines told me to do."

Dahlberg's Diving Minnow
(Larry Dahlberg)
Hook: Tiemco 9394, sizes 4-1/o
Tail: White marabou; silver, pearl Flashabou; grizzly hackle, blue, purple
Body: Silver braided Mylar
Collar: Deer hair, white, black
Head: White deer hair
Weedguard: Mason hard mono 20-pound
Notes: This is the silver version. Other colors include black, darter, golden, perch. Available wholesale from Umpqua Feather Merchants.

Dahlberg's Rabbit Strip Diver
(Larry Dahlberg)
Hook: Tiemco 811S, sizes 4 and 1
Tail: Chartreuse rabbit strip; gold Flashabou
Body: Cross cut rabbit strip, chartreuse
Collar: Deer hair, chartreuse
Head: Chartreuse deer hair
Weedguard: Mason hard mono 20-pound
Notes: This is the chartreuse version. Other colors

include black, olive, white, yellow. Available from The Fly Shop and wholesale from Umpqua Feather Merchants.

One of the most effective variations of Larry's first design was to substitute a rabbit strip tail for the marabou and hackle tips. One of the keys to the effectiveness of the deer hair collar is that it changes the water flow around the fly. When you retrieve it, or when it's swimming in moving water, the collar creates a vortex, a space behind the collar that helps create a bubble chain of oxygen bubbles. That attracts fish and makes the fly seem alive. The rabbit strip tail tends to

kick around in that bubble chain, further enhancing the effectiveness of this fly.

Larry says, "You make the tail very long and of soft materials. I like rabbit and Flashabou because it gets soaked up real good. When you pull it, the fly gets shorter, and when you slow it down, the fly gets longer—because the vortex that the head makes causes the tail to get sucked up. If you tie the tail too short, it won't even run because the whole tail gets sucked up in the vortex. You have to make it long enough to escape that vortex."

EdgeWater's Dive-in Minnow
(EdgeWater)

Hook: Stinger, sizes 1/0 and 2
Tail: Marabou; pearl Flashabou
Body: Foam
Eyes: Solid plastic, black on yellow
Weedguard: Plastic coated wire loops
Notes: This is the black version. Others are yellow, purple, white, blue, chartreuse. Available from EdgeWater, who also sell the foam heads.

Kruger's Desperate Diver
(Ron Kruger)

Hook: Mustad kink-shank popper, size 1
Tail: Squirrel tail; silver Flashabou
Body: Black braid; cork
Wing: Black deer hair
Gills: Red chenille
Eyes: Doll eyes, black on white
Notes: This is the regular version; the Magnum has a rabbit-strip tail. This is the black; other colors are silver (shad), rust (crayfish), chartreuse, white, and peppered olive (frog). Former bass guide Ron Kruger, of Benton, Kentucky brings years of experience fishing conventional gear for bass to the world of fly fishing. In fact, for two years Ron fly fished side-by-side with bass fishermen using spinnerbaits, jig-and-pigs, and stickbaits. He says, "In those two years, there was only one time that I didn't do just as well as the guys using conventional bass gear.

"I designed the Desperate Diver as the fly fisherman's Rapala, and it is deadly on bass in shallow water—water less than six feet deep. The reversed cork head causes the fly to dive when retrieved, and the large

bulging eyes cause it to wobble while adding a sense of wild-eyed fear that game fish find so irresistible. The selection of natural materials (calf tail, squirrel tail and deer hair) creates a realistic baitfish silhouette and action that plastic can't match. The red throat represents the exposed gills of an excited fish. And the tinsel adds attention-getting flash, which not only glitters when the fly is pulled under, but waves seductively as it swims back to the surface.

"These colors were developed partly to mimic the general coloration of various forage and partly because bass are color specific at certain times. No bass fisherman would be without chartreuse baits—and neither should the fly fisherman for bass. Experiment with the various colors. If you'll notice, they're a spectrum of shades, from white to black. As a general rule, try the lighter colors when the sky is bright, the darker colors as the light fades."

Ron designed the Desperate Diver for a fast retrieve, triggering bass to strike fleeing prey. Use quick, short strips without pausing.

He says, "Desperate Divers not only incorporate a unique design, they were designed to be fished in a manner somewhat unique to fly fishing. In a word: aggressively. Or in other words, don't fish them like a fly or popper. Fish them like a lure.

"Forget about casting it out and letting all the rings disappear before you move it. Forget about using the slight twitch of a popper, or the gentle pull of the slider or deer-hair diver. Instead, start them back the instant it hits the water. Jerk it under aggressively, and, the second it pops back up, jerk it back under again. This is exactly the manner in which a Rapala is twitched on the surface. Some fans of the Desperate Diver like to pause

it briefly between jerks, but most swear that the faster you fish it, the more fish attack it.

"Hold your rod tip low and slightly to one side. Aggressively strip line and jerk the rod tip at the same time. You want the Diver to make as much commotion as possible in the shortest area, so instead of making the Diver dive by pulling it under, simply slap the slack out of the fly line to twitch it under. This causes the Desperate Diver to burst into a dive that pulls air bubbles under. When done properly, the Diver will make a gurgling noise with each dive and will only move forward a few inches at a time. Try to develop a rhythm, stripping line and twitch the rod tip on a count of one-second intervals.

"Such a presentation is so productive because it appeals to a bass's predator instincts. Like the design of most baitcasting lures, fishing a Desperate Diver this way brings instinct strikes from fish that may not be particularly hungry. This presentation gives the impression that the Diver is alive, injured, and frantically "Desperately" trying to escape. It looks like an easy capture, but the bass is forced to make up its mind quickly—its instincts kick in and the surface explodes." Desperate Divers patented and available from Krugercraft (see Sources, page 130).

Mark's Fire Tiger Diver
(Mark Sturtevant)

Hook: Mustad 3366
Thread: Hot orange flat waxed nylon
Tail: Fluorescent lime green Zonker strip; fluorescent orange marabou; black Flashabou
Skirt: Chartreuse Estaz
Collar: Fluorescent orange deer belly hair
Head: Fluorescent chartreuse, black, fluorescent orange deer belly hair
Notes: Mark Sturtevant, of Scotland, Pennsylvania says, "I developed my Fire Tiger patterns as a result of my years of experience as a professional bass guide and tournament angler on the tidal Potomac River and waters throughout the eastern US. During my years of conventional tackle bass angling, I found the Fire Tiger

crankbaits to be exceptionally productive lures in lakes, reservoirs and tidal rivers from Vermont to Florida. As I turned primarily to fly fishing, it was only natural that I developed Fire Tiger bass bugs." (see Sources, page 130)

Rabe's Bloody Undertaker
Dave Rabe)

Hook: Kink shank popper, size 1/0
Tail: Black ram's wool; 8 black saddle hackles
Collar: Black saddle (three)
Cheeks: Guinea dyed red
Body: Black foam
Legs: Black rubber strands
Eyes: Solid plastic, black on orange
Notes: This is the black version. Others are white, olive, yellow. Dave Rabe of Milford, Ohio says, "This is the most versatile foam fly I use. In still water it will slide or dive, depending on the retrieve. In moving water it will dive and wiggle when fished on a tight-line,

streamer retrieve. It also has the distinction of nosing into the bottom, and either floating or bouncing over obstructions."

Sanchez Prism Diver
(Scott Sanchez)

Hook: Dai-Riki 930 stainless, 1 x-strong, standard length, sizes 2 to 3/0
Thread: White Flymaster or Monocord size A
Tail: Rabbit strip, chinchilla, silicone caulking, glitter; holographic silver strands; rubber legs, white
Body: Deer hair, natural
Rear Collar: Deer hair, natural
Diving Collar: Red foam; silver prism tape attached
Gills: Red deer hair
Eyes: Molded plastic, black on yellow
Head: Natural deer hair; optional, top, mottled with black deer hair
Weedguard: Mason hard mono 20-pound

Notes: This is the white version; others include black, gray, chartreuse. Scott Sanchez, of Livingston, Montana says, "The great thing about divers is that they are both a surface and a subsurface fly. This makes it a great fly to fish in varying conditions. I wanted to make the diver float longer when it gets waterlogged—hopefully by fish—and to improve its underwater appearance.

"The Prism Diver is a modification of the Dahlberg Diver. A stiff-glue-reinforced collar on the Dahlberg Diver causes it to push more water than an unstiffened collar. To make the glued collar look the best it is usually glued when the collar is still rough and given a final trim when the collar is dry. This can be time consuming.

"The idea for the foam/prism tape collar came while bass fishing in east Texas and was tested almost

immediately with good results. Pike, snook, stripers and magnum sunfish like to include it in their diet, also. The Prism Diver has worked extremely well on stripers chasing shad on top. I have even managed to catch four species of trout on it.

"The foam makes the fly stay at the surface when you want it there and the partially saturated (with water) deer hair makes it dive well. The lure tape gives it a crankbait look under water. I like to fish this fly as a popper along bankside vegetation and as it moves to open water, pull it underneath as a streamer. I've caught numerous fish on this fly subsurface. My biggest bass on this fly was around six pounds.

"I generally tie this fly on Dai-Riki 930 stainless hooks. This allows me to fish them in fresh or salt water and to not lose a fly from a rusted hook when I forgot and put my flies away wet. This heavier wire helps to ballast the fly, also. In the smaller sizes I will tie a tail of Wing Fiber (synthetic)."

Skip's Fusion Bug
(Skip Morris)

Hook: Tiemco 8089, size 10

Tail: 3 to 5 strands round rubber, small, black and yellow; splayed yellow grizzly hackle

Rear Collar: Black closed-cell foam

Body: Yellow deer, elk or antelope hair

Legs: Two pair strands round rubber, small, black and yellow

Notes: This is the yellow and black version, although you can tie other colors to suit. In his book, *The Art of Tying the Bass Fly*, 1996, where he describes tying and fishing this fly, Skip wrote, "This isn't my first pattern for a diving bass fly, but I believe it is my best. My first was the Morrisfoam Diver, whose tying I described in *Tying Foam Flies*, 1994. The Morrisfoam Diver remains a useful, effective pattern, and of the two, it is the quickest and easiest to tie.

"But the Skip's Fusion Bug makes the very best use of its two most significant materials—deer hair and foam. The front end of a diving fly should ride low, keep its nose tucked a bit, ready for a downward lunge; the deer-hair (or elk-hair or antelope-hair) body of the Fusion Bug soaks up enough water to do this duty well indeed. Yet no matter how sodden the deer becomes, the foam holds everything afloat. The foam's lightness and buoyancy also tend to right the fly should it land upside down or on its side."

Skip's Hover Bug
(Skip Morris)

Hook: Stinger hook, size 10

Tail: Rabbit strip, hide up; loop of 10-pound Maxima; gold Krystal Flash

Rear Collar: Closed-cell foam, gray

Body: Closed-cell foam, gray

Legs: Black round rubber, small

Eyes: Doll eyes, black on yellow

Notes: This is the gray version; Skip also likes the all-black version. Use other colors to suit.

Skip usually fishes it on a full-sink line. The loop of stiff monofilament to keep the rabbit strip from fouling the hook is innovative: put a hard crimp in a loop of mono, thread it through two holes in the rabbit and tie the ends down under the body/collar area. The loop is installed about halfway back on the rabbit strip, which keeps the rabbit out away from the bend in the hook, but still allows for good hook-setting. Find the details and step-by-step color photos in Skip's book, *The Art of Tying the Bass Fly*, 1996.

He says, "Nearly always I fish it well down, actively, with brief pauses. I keep it active because detecting a bass's take can be very difficult on a slow retrieve of the fly—a bass can mouth a fly without even moving it. But if a bass touches an active fly, the angler will see or feel the resistance.

"To best fish the Skip's Hover Bug, play with it, and observe. Let the line take it down a few inches. Its supple tail undulates softly, long after the rest of the fly is still. Tug the line—the rubber-strands sweep back, then slowly swing outwards. Make the fly move in quick pulses; the legs and tail respond differently than before, yet are still lively. Now you can see, in your mind, the movement of the fly as you work it over the bottom. That's always an advantage."

Stewart's Lucky Wiggler
(Jim Stewart)

Hook: Stinger, size 1/0

Tail: Rubber strands, orange, yellow, chartreuse; chartreuse, yellow grizzly hackle; chartreuse Krystal Flash; silver Flashabou

Rear Collar: Hot pink chenille; chartreuse deer hair

Body: Deer hair, chartreuse, yellow, white, orange

Eyes: Plastic, black on white

Weedguard: Double hard mono loops

Notes: This the green/orange head; others include white/red head; yellow; black, purple, blue/red head. Jim Stewart of Tampa, Florida was a fly fisherman and tier from Tennessee who found Florida waters to be ideal for fly rodding, but was frustrated that standard poppers didn't work as well as baitcasting plugs.

In *Bassmaster* magazine, March 1992, Bob McNally quoted Stewart: "Most flies have actions according to how the angler works the fly line during the retrieve. But plug flies have built-in actions like plugs. You throw out a plug and it does something other than just come straight in. A plug fly, when pulled in, will dive. It will pop. It will wiggle. It will pop and dive and wiggle. It will go deep, run shallow, do all the things that various plugs do for baitcasting anglers. And when the retrieve is paused, plug flies will rise to the surface much like floating-diving plugs."

Stewart uses the shapes that have made traditional plugs so effective. He says, "The degree of forward slope on a plug fly's face produces the action I desire. For example, a bill almost horizontal or in line with the hook eye will make the artificial dive deeply. Same thing is true with a plug fly. The lower the diving angle in the deer-hair face, the deeper the plug fly will run during the retrieve. The sharper the diving angle in the face, the quicker it will dive—but it won't continue to go down because deer hair is buoyant. I have achieved these different things with plug flies, only I have used spun deer hair instead of wood or plastic."

Of the Lucky Wiggler, McNally wrote: "The bug's name comes from two old lure favorites of Stewart's youthful bassing days—the Heddon Lucky 13 and the Hawaiian Wiggler. The Lucky Wiggler has a flat face but with a horizontal bill at the hook eye that makes it pop and/or dive during the retrieve much like the old Lucky 13. Stewart frequently ties the Lucky Wiggler with a rubber skirt, which gives it an action much like the old Hawaiian Wiggler—the first lure he remembers having a rubber skirt. When popped and then retrieved underwater, this plug fly creates a very long stream bubbles, which is well known among serious BASSers to draw predator game fish from long distances."

In *Outdoor Life*, May 1993, Jerry Gibbs wrote, "This extremely versatile bug can be popped and, followed by a short-strip retrieve, will dive with the tail working and head wobbling slightly, side to side. A powerful strip brings the Lucky Wiggler down eight inches in a straight dive and swim. For spooky fish, anglers can omit the popping and simply perform a swim/dive retrieve. According to Stewart, the bug imitates a minnow feeding near the surface, then fleeing." Available wholesale from Umpqua Feather Merchants. Jim Stewart ties for collectors (see Sources, page 130).

Stewart's Chub Darter
(Jim Stewart)

Hook: Long-shank stainless-steel hook, sizes 1/0, 2, 6

Tail: Green grizzly hackle; green Flashabou, silver Krystal Flash

Rear Collar: Hot pink chenille; deer hair, natural, green, black

Body: Deer hair, natural, green, black

Eyes: Plastic, black on white

Weedguard: Double hard mono loops

Notes: This is the green-back version; others include white/red head; blue back; chartreuse/orange head. In *Bassmaster* magazine, March 1992, Bob McNally wrote, "This plug/fly was inspired by an old baitcasting plug, the Creek Chub Darter. The bug performs during the retrieve much like the old Creek Chub plug. The fly has an offset cup face and a diving lip. It will dive deeply, or it can be worked with short twitches that cause the fly to zigzag just under the water's surface. This bug performs best when it is kept moving, and is therefore ideal for blind casting around bass cover."

In *Outdoor Life*, May 1993, Jerry Gibbs wrote, "Like the original Chub Creek Darter or any minnow-type lure, this bug is worked teasingly on the surface. Alternating short strips and pauses will produce a walk-the-dog motion, as when fishing a Zara Spook. A strong, sharp strip causes the bug plug to dive—sometimes out of sight.

"This is a bug worth using anytime minnows are showering from the water escaping a predator. When fish are showing, Stewart likes to work the Chub Darter on the surface until he feels he has the fish's attention. Then he suddenly makes the bug dive. The Chub Darter has less action when at rest than the Lucky Wiggler, but it's designed to be worked more aggressively and presents a sleek minnow profile when it is."

Gibbs quotes Stewart: "I like to work the Chub Darter faster than other bugs. It's a good one for a novice, too, because when it's being worked correctly the line is kept tight, unlike a popper which produces a little slack after it is popped."

Stewart's Jointed Bass-A-Roo
(Jim Stewart)

Hook: Stinger, size 2
Tail: White bucktail; grizzly hackle; red Krystal Flash; silver Flashabou
Jointed Collar: Red grizzly hackle
Rear Collar: Hot pink chenille; deer hair, white, red
Body: Deer hair, white, red, black
Eyes: Large plastic, black on blue
Weedguard: Double hard mono loops
Notes: This is the white version; others include yellow; frog; chartreuse; black, purple, blue with red head; black, rust; natural. Jim Stewart designed this jointed plug/fly to mimic a quick-diving Creek Chub Pikie; the

single-body configuration mimics the old Heddon River Runt or Bass Oreno plug.

Stewart's Hair Spoon
(Jim Stewart)

Hook: Stinger, size 6
Tail: Rubber strands, white, chartreuse, blue
Body: Deer hair, white, chartreuse
Eyes: Plastic, black on white
Weedguard: Double hard mono loops
Notes: This is the white version; others include yellow; frog. Designed to simulate a wobbling, weedless spoon for heavy cover.

Floating Divers

Stewart's Dying Side Winder
(Jim Stewart)

Hook: Stinger, sizes 1/0, 2
Tail: Grizzly hackle; gray marabou
Rear Collar: Deer hair, white
Rear Eyes: Solid black plastic
Body: Deer hair, white, red, blue
Eyes: Plastic, black on blue
Weedguard: Double hard mono loops
Notes: This is the shad version; others include shiner and bluegill.

Sublett's Fuzzy Leg Frog
(Randy Sublett)

Hook: Mustad 3407, size 2/0
Collar: Deer hair, yellow, olive, black
Body: Deer hair, yellow, olive, black
Legs: Rabbit strips, yellow
Eyes: Doll eyes, black on yellow

Sublett's Shad Diver
(Randy Sublett)

Hook: Mustad 3407, size 2/0
Tail: Black rubber legs
Collar: Deer hair, black, white
Body: Deer hair, black, white, gray
Eyes: Doll eyes, black on yellow

Tullis Wiggle Snake
(Larry Tullis)

Hook: Tiemco stinger, size 2, front; Daiichi 2461, size 2, rear
Tail: Black marabou; pearl Krystal Flash
Body: Black foam tubes
Head: Wiggle Bug foam; black Estaz; black hackle
Eyes: Painted, black on yellow
Weedguard: Stainless steel wire loop, bent
Notes: Larry says he designed this fly for big bass. Available from Larry Tullis (see Sources, page 130).

Hot Bass Flies

Ty's Tantalizer
(Tim England)

Hook: Tiemco 8089, sizes 2 to 6; Mustad AC80300BR, sizes 2 to 10

Thread: Dynacord (UNI-Cord) 3/0, Gudebrod G

Tail: Splayed capon rooster hackle; round rubber; flash material (optional)

Body: Rear, over tail tie-down, Estaz or similar material, color to match fly; stacked whitetail deer hair, color to suit tier

Collar: Whitetail deer hair, color to suit tier

Eyes: Solid plastic, 4 1/2 to 6mm

Notes: Tied by Chris Helm, who says, "I usually do not put a weedguard on this pattern since I fish it in open water. Fishing a diver in the middle of a weed patch, lily pads, etc. just leads to problems getting hung up. Ty's Tantalizer works well for bass and is also a good pattern for pike. If used for pike I tie in a three-inch rabbit strip for the tail or use saltwater saddle hackle about three inches long and a good amount of Flashabou or other flash material.

"The reason I like it better than a Dahlberg Diver is that the design eliminates the likelihood of it flipping over after it becomes waterlogged. You'll note that there is quite a bit of hair below the hook shank. It is also tied just on the front half of the hook shank. Combined with the hook bend this makes the fly very well balanced and it stays upright. Also, I always grease my hair bugs with a good-quality fly floatant." Chris sells this fly retail, special order. Chris ties the Ty's Tantalizer in his newest video, "Tying Hair Bugs with Chris Helm" (see Sources, page 130).

Umpqua's Swimming Baitfish
(Umpqua Feather Merchants)

Hook: Tiemco 811S, size 1/0

Tail: Krystal Flash, silver, pearl; white hackle; grizzly hackle

Gills: Red Flashabou

Collar: Deer hair, natural

Head: Deer hair, white, natural, orange, red

Eyes: Plastic, black on gold

Weedguard: Mason hard mono 20-pound

Notes: This is the red/white version. Others include the red/yellow; shad. Available wholesale from Umpqua Feather Merchants.

Umpqua's Swimming Frog
(Umpqua Feather Merchants)

Hook: Stinger, Tiemco 8089, sizes 2 and 6

Tail: Orange Krystal Flash; orange hackle; grizzly hackle, orange, yellow, olive

Legs: Rubber strands, orange, green, chartreuse

Collar: Deer hair, orange, black, chartreuse

Head: Deer hair, orange, black, chartreuse

Eyes: Plastic, black on white

Weedguard: Mason hard mono 20-pound

Notes: This is the Orange Belly version. Others include the White Belly and Yellow Belly. When bass are feeding in shallow water, this swimming/diving frog is

absolutely deadly. Available from The Fly Shop and wholesale from Umpqua Feather Merchants.

Walega's M.R. Live Diver
(Michael R. Walega)

Hook: Mustad 3407, size 2/0
Tail: White Hairabou; pearl Krystal Flash
Body: 3/4-inch-diameter Live Body Foam, white
Eyes: Doll eyes, black on yellow
Notes: Available through Michael R. Walega, M.R. Flies.

Wiggle Bug
(Steve Shiba/Larry Tullis)

Hook: Daiichi 2461, sizes 4/0-6
Tail: Marabou
Body: Foam; Crystal Chenille
Legs: Palmered hackle (on 2/0 and 4/0 only)
Eyes: Solid plastic, black on yellow
Notes: This is the blue/white version. Others are yellow, white, black, chartreuse, purple, black/chartreuse. Available from EdgeWater and Larry Tullis (see Sources). Kits or the foam bodies are available. Closely related are the Wiggle Damsel and Wiggle Nymph.

Wiggle Craw
(Steve Shiba/Larry Tullis)

Hook: Daiichi 2461, sizes 2/0, 2, 6
Antennae: Rubber legs, deer hair
Body: Foam; permanent marker; Crystal Chenille
Legs: Palmered hackle
Eyes: Black pin heads
Weight: Lead in diving lip
Notes: Available from EdgeWater and Larry Tullis.

Wiggle Critter
(Steve Shiba/Larry Tullis)

Hook: Stinger
Tail: Marabou; hackle; Krystal Flash
Body: Foam
Eyes: Painted, black on yellow
Notes: The Wiggle Critter is a cross between a Dive-in Minnow and a Wiggle Bug; it dives and its action is a little tighter than the Wiggle Bug. The Wiggle Critter is available from EdgeWater or Larry Tullis (see Sources). Both sell the foam heads.

54

Bill Black of Spirit River enjoys researching bass flies.

Floating Divers

Dan Lynch guides Carey Marcus in the timber at Lake Fork, Texas.

Hot Bass Flies

Floating Critters

Bass will eat an incredible variety of foods—fish, crayfish, worms, tadpoles, salamanders, frogs, and bugs of all types. Bass are equally democratic about taking an incredible variety of flies.

Fly-flingers seem to have an undeniable urge to relate all flies to some kind of naturally occurring critter, and bassers are no exception. Obviously, bass feed on natural stuff or there wouldn't be any bass at which to fling. But bass also attack things that resemble nothing they've eaten before. In many instances, a fly must excite a bass to strike, not resemble a normal food item.

These critter flies presented here reflect that propensity for fly tiers and fly fishermen to tie and fish stuff that bears a resemblance to nature. (Non-floating critters are included in the Subsurface chapter, page 130?.)

Barr's Floating Dragonfly Nymph
(John Barr)

Hook: Tiemco 8089 size 10
Tail: Black marabou; black Krystal Flash
Body: Black deer hair
Legs: Black soft hackle
Wingpad: Clear Mylar sheeting
Collar: Black Estaz
Head: Black Estaz
Eyes: Doll eyes, black on yellow

Barr's Paint Your Dragon
(John Barr)

Hook: Tiemco 8089 size 10
Tail: White foam
Body: White foam
Wing: Gray bucktail
Head: White foam
Notes: This white foam version allows you to match the color of the prevalent dragonfly with a permanent marker, especially when traveling to unknown waters. You can also trim it a bit to mimic damselflies.

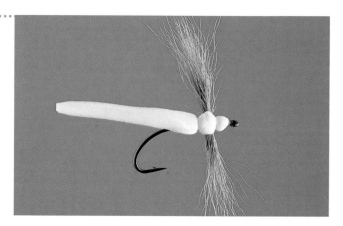

Burk's Basshopper
(Andy Burk)

Hook: Tiemco 2312, size 6
Underwing: Red deer hair; pearl Krystal Flash
Wing: Brown turkey tail or synthetic substitute
Collar: Deer hair
Legs: Rear, round yellow rubber knotted with black spots; front, round yellow rubber
Body: Yellow deer hair
Head: Deer hair

Pobst's Keel Grasshopper
(Dick Pobst)

Hook: Mustad keel hook, size 6
Tail: Red hackle fibers; tips of yellow deer hair body
Body: Yellow deer hair palmered with brown hackle
Wing: Mallard dyed wood duck; natural deer hair
Head: Natural deer hair
Notes: This is the grasshopper version. Another is an all-yellow version for the big yellow mayfly (*Hexagenia limbata*). Available from Thornapple Orvis Shop (see Sources, page 130).

Sanchez Convertible Damselfly
(Scott Sanchez)

Hook: Dai-Riki 270, sizes 8 to 14
Thread: Blue 6/o
Tail: Blue bucktail, one hook shank length
Body: Blue dubbing, rear half of hook shank
Legs: Blue rubber
Down Wing: Gray calf tail, extends to rear half of tail length
Up Wings: Split to form "V", from stubs of down wing
Hackle: Grizzly, one and a half hook gape in diameter
Notes: Scott Sanchez of Livingston, Montana says, "The Convertible Damselfly is a variation of my original Convertible. The double-wing profile simulates the fluttering wings of the adult damsel on the water. An effective summer pattern for trout and warmwater species. It is a great fly for bass and sunfish on lakes and moving water. Try an occasional twitch to entice the fish."

The Dan Bailey catalog states, "The Convertible Series is another innovation courtesy of Scott Sanchez and the Jackson Hole One-Fly contest. With both a down wing and upright wings, these flies represent different species of insects. With a quick snip of the scissors one of the wings can be removed for a more realistic impression."

Smith's Dirty Bird
(Harry Smith)

Hook: Tiemco, size 2 Stinger
Tail: Black feather, fluffy; natural deer hair
Body: Grizzly feathers, fluffy
Legs: Flat rubber, knotted, then splayed out for feet, pale chartreuse
Wings: Grizzly feathers, fluffy
Back: Black feather, fluffy
Collar: Rust deer hair
Head: Rust and black deer hair
Eyes: Solid plastic, black on amber
Notes: This is one version; the other is gray and white instead of rust and black, and it has dark green legs. Harry Smith of Santa Ana devised this unique fly for fishing the half-sunken trees and brush surrounding Southern California's Oso Reservoir.

Harry says, "It's a sort of match-the-hatch thing. I got to thinking what do I see flying around, what are flies made of, why are the bass so deep back in the brush, what hatches in the spring time? Birds! A bird flopping in the water struggles to find a limb to climb out. My fishing method is with a 12-weight rod and three to six inches of 25-pound leader hanging from the tip. I have teeth marks on my rod to attest to the success of this method. I do not recommend this technique to the weak and feeble of heart. I do recommend it to those who want to venture out on a limb and sit there with the Dirty Bird. Sometimes the wait is not too long."

Frank Dawley of Big Bluff Ranch in Northern California told me that an angler fishing for bass in his Sweetwater Lake caught a four-pound bass with a partially digested blackbird in its stomach—and some of its feathers were sticking out of the fish's mouth.

Bramlett Branham of Raleigh, South Carolina told me this story: "We were standing out by a cypress pond early in the morning when the female wood ducks were bringing the young ducklings out of three nests to swim around in the pond for the first time. The mother ducks coaxed them to jump from about ten to fifteen feet above the water; they would hit the water with a slap. The big bass would come up and just take one of them when they hit the water. And then after the mother swims off with the little babies trailing behind her, you can see the big bass following the whole procession of ducks and coming up and sipping the last one in line.

"We tied up something we thought would look like a wood duck, a brown hair bug, clipped pronghorn antelope hair with a tail and two orange grizzly hackles hanging off the bottom, a real rough looking fly.

"We'd make a big, high cast and let this thing slap the water as hard as it can, and the bass would come up and hammer it." Bramlett says he got a six-pounder and some other ones, but never could get into position to nail the bass eating the last baby in the procession behind mom duck. He also says that several years ago an angler showed him a four-pound bass with a hummingbird in its stomach. Bramblett says hummingbirds feed on the nectar in the lily pad blossoms (although that particular fish succumbed to a plastic worm).

Spirit River's Giant Blue Dragon
(Spirit River)

Hook: Stinger, sizes 6 and 10
Tail: Blue foam
Body: Blue foam
Wing: White Super Hair
Head: Blue foam
Eyes: Black mono
Weedguard: Mason hard mono 20-pound
Notes: Available wholesale from Spirit River.

Stewart's Dragon Moth
(Jim Stewart)

Hook: Stinger, size 2
Tail: Mated goose feather, Accent Flash
Body: Crystal chenille, deer hair
Wing: Deer hair
Collar: Deer hair
Head: Deer hair
Eyes: Black plastic
Notes: This is the red version; others include blue, olive. Available wholesale from Umpqua Feather Merchants. Jim Stewart ties for collectors (see Sources).

Walega's M.R. Bugly
(Michael R. Walega)

Hooks: Rear, Mustad 36620 size 10 (6 x-long ring eye); front, Mustad 36620 size 6 (6 x-long ring eye)
Tail Collar: Grizzly hackle
Rear Body: #90 Ant Body; continuation of tail; permanent marker, black spots on top
Front Body: #175 Ant Body; permanent marker, black spots on top
Hinge: .011 stainless wire (#2)
Legs: Large square black rubber
Eyes: Doll eyes, black on white
Notes: Available through Michael R. Walega, M.R. Flies (see Sources, page 130).

Walega's M.R. Snakes
(Michael R. Walega)

Hooks: Mustad 9674 size 4 (4x-long ring eye)
Tail: Black rabbit strip (4 inches or less)
Rear Body: #175 Ant Body; continuation of tail
Front Body: Large Spider Body reversed
Hinge: .011 stainless wire (#2)
Eyes: Doll eyes, black on white
Notes: Available through Michael R. Walega, M.R. Flies
(see Sources, page 130).

Yamagata's Extended Dragonfly
(Jeff Yamagata)

Hook: Tiemco 8089, sizes 2-10
Abdomen: 30-pound mono; closed-cell foam, light green,
   olive
Body: Green deer hair or dubbing
Legs: Olive silicone strands or Super Floss
Wing: Poly Yarn, pearl Krystal Flash
Wingpads: Green closed-cell foam; black permanent
   marker; glitter
Head: Same as body
Eyes: Solid plastic, black on amber
Notes: Available at A-1 Fish Fly Fishing Supplies (see
   Sources, page 130).

Open Clinch Knot

For maximum movement, all bass flies should be attached with an open-style knot. For some to swim properly, such as the Betts Bull-It Head and the Wiggle Bug, you must use an open-style knot.

1. Put overhand knot in tippet but leave open.

2. Put tippet through hook eye.

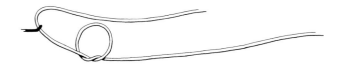

3. Wrap tippet around itself 5 times.

4. Run end of tippet through overhand knot and loop formed by twisted tippet.

5. Pinch knot at distance desired from hook eye.

Jeff Hull hauls out a largemouth at Upsata Lake, Montana.

Hot Bass Flies

Chapter 5

Fly-Rod Spinnerbaits

Whether you use Andy Burk's Bass Flash or spinnerbaits with metal blades, adding this type of design to your arsenal will allow you to catch bass when nothing else works. Because presentation of spinnerbaits varies radically, from super-slow to super-fast, you can appeal to bass in almost any mood.

Over forty years ago, conventional bass folks hit on the idea of combining a jig-and-spinner cluster that proved absolutely deadly on largemouth. Perhaps bass see the spinner/jig as food, or maybe they react as aggressive, territorial predators. At any rate, with a super-fast retrieve, the spinnerbait allowed bassers to cover lots of water, triggering bass to launch themselves from cover when they wouldn't respond to conventional lures.

Bassers soon discovered that largemouth found the sinking spinnerbait, with its blades barely twirling as it sank, to be irresistible. The spinnerbait became a must-have in the bass master's tackle box—a lure that could be ripped through the water to trigger fish-attacks, or dropped off ledges and structure in a strike-enticing free fall.

In his 1968 book, *Fly Tying and Fly Fishing for Bass and Panfish*, Tom Nixon wrote about constructing spinnerbaits with metal blades and fishing them with a fly rod. Fly flingers now have a half-century tradition of tossing spinnerbaits. However, this tradition is actually an extension of the standard fly-rod tactic of casting a fly and spinner combo that dates back to the earliest days of fly fishing in this country, as chronicled in Henshall's *Book of the Black Bass*, 1883, 1923. In his 1925 book, *The Fly-Rod for Bass*, Cal Johnson wrote about using fly-rod lures, which included fly/spinner combos, cork-bodied and deer-hair flies, as well as "fly rod wigglers, miniature replicas of the larger bait casting plugs." In his 1958 book, *Complete Book of Fly Fishing*, Joe Brooks included a chart for "Patterns for fly and spinner combinations."

Burk's Bass Flash
(Andy Burk)

Hook: Stinger, sizes 2-10
Wing: Silver Flashabou
Armature: 15# hard Mason monofilament (can substitute 25# Maxima Chameleon)
Legs: Lime with black specks (Sili Legs)
Body: Fluorescent red chenille butt; white chenille
Eyes: Various weighted eyes lead, nickel-plated, non-toxic with pupil
Weedguard: Mason hard monofilament, 15# for size 10, 20# for size 6, 25# for size 2
Notes: Options include a rabbit-strip tail; enclosed rattle; black chenille, gold Flashabou for stained water; other color combinations. Available from The Fly Shop and wholesale from Umpqua Feather Merchants (see Sources, page 130).

In 1992, Andy Burk of Reno, Nevada, designed his version of the spinnerbait using conventional fly tying materials; stiff monofilament forms the armature and Flashabou simulates the blades. Chenille locks the Sili legs in place, making them radiate out from the fly. In some flies he adds a rattle to create underwater noise when the fly bangs into structure, adding to the fly's effectiveness at night or in murky water. His Bass Flash tied with a rabbit strip trailer is particularly deadly as it sinks.

He says, "On the sink, it's an Inhaler Fly—all you see is the silver Flashabou and the rabbit strip—the rest is in the fish's mouth."

The Burk's Bass Flash is versatile: you can fish it on a floating or sinking line and vary your tactics. Andy says, "My favorite type of water to fish it is among fallen timber. Closely watch the fly line as the fly sinks. A lot of times the fish hammer it as it sinks into their lair. You can swim it back past a tree trunk or cast it right up against the shoreline and swim it back.

"When you look at how spinnerbaits are fished by conventional fishermen, they're fished extremely fast. On a floating line in shallow water, particularly with fallen timber or along a steep drop-off bank, I'll let the fly fall, and then begin a fairly fast retrieve, with two-foot pulls. If I hold the rod high, I can make it "V" along the surface, just like a spinnerbait.

"With a sinking line, I'll cast the fly out on a short leader (four to six feet), make sure the line is straight, hold the rod tip low, with the line over my finger, and I watch very carefully as the fly sinks. A lot of times the fish will hit it as the fly falls. I start with fast four to six inch pulls, then just steady, long pulls that bounce the fly off cover and the bottom contours. This fly has that seductive appearance, and even when you stop moving the fly, the fly is still moving because those silicone legs will not pause—they are always in motion."

Fly Rod Spinnerbait
(Meyer version, Fire Tiger)

Hook: Jig hook, sizes 6 to 4/0 (Daiichi 4660, Mustad 32741BR, 32742BR)
Tail: Rabbit strip (two strips, separated) chartreuse
Body: Rattle under black chenille and chartreuse Estaz
Legs: Sili Legs, fire tiger (orange speckled, lime speckled and chartreuse)
Wing: Silver Flashabou
Armature: 15# hard Mason monofilament (can substitute 25# Maxima Chameleon
Eyes: Real Eyes with insert
Notes: Based on Burk's Bass Flash, this fire tiger version is one of my favorites. I prefer the jig-style hook with no weedguard. Another variation is a double armature with

Flashabou setup, helpful when working heavy cover. (For tying instructions, see my book *Tying Bass Flies: 12 of the Best.*)

Knight's Fly Rod Spinnerbait
(Ron Knight)

Hook: Mustad 3366, size 4
Armature: Bent and looped metal, swivel, ring, hammered silver blade
Tail: Silicone strands, purple with black flecks
Body: Light blue Crystal Chenille
Collar: Silicone strands, purple with black flecks
Head: Black thread
Eyes: Painted, black on orange on chartreuse
Notes: This is the purple version. Ron Knight of Leavenworth, Kansas likes white with fluorescent yellow, black with white, and others, and size 1 and 2/0.

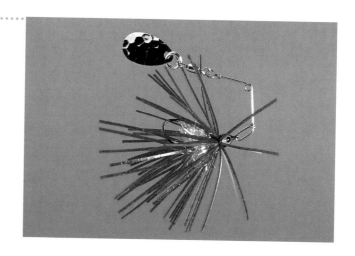

Nixon's Black & White Fly Rod Spinnerbait
(Tom Nixon)

Hook: Mustad 3366, size 2/0
Armature: Bent and looped metal, swivel, ring, silver blade
Tail: White rubber strands
Body: Fat black chenille
Hackle: Black palmered
Collar: Black rubber strands
Head: Black thread
Eyes: Painted, red on yellow
Notes: Tom Nixon of Lake Charles, Louisiana tied this spinnerbait in March, 1998 while in his 80s. A trailblazer in what some regard as non-conventional methods with a fly rod, Tom's book *Fly Tying and Fly Fishing for Bass and Panfish*, 1968, 1977, still holds many truths for those wanting to catch bass. Ironically, using the long rod for flies, as well as bait, lures, and flies coupled with spinners, dates back to the nineteenth century, well before what many now view as the "traditional" way to use the fly rod—with flies and poppers only.

Sally Childears battles a bass at Barnes Butte Lake, Oregon.

One reason the Woolly Bugger is so effective on bass is that, among other things, it resembles a crayfish.

Crayfish

Smallmouth are particularly fond of flies with rubber legs—possibly because the rubber fronds seem like crayfish feelers and rear legs.

It's accepted fact that bass crave crayfish, and bass love to gobble young crayfish in one bite. As a reflection of this propensity, most crayfish flies imitate a fully-formed but juvenile crawdad about two inches long.

However, while fishing the clear water of the Umpqua River in Oregon at the Big K Ranch in mid-summer, I discovered several things I hadn't realized. Since even good-sized smallmouth can seldom engulf adult crayfish, bass crunch up the victim, and crawdad parts are strewn about the dining area. In addition, when bass see one of their brethren scarfing a 'dad, they zoom in to take part in the feast. Not only do the newly arrived bass try to steal the already crunched crawdad, they also feed on the bits and pieces floating downstream. Furthermore, a hooked smallmouth will often spit out crawdad crumbs, which other bass will immediately consume.

I also discovered that although the outside of the crayfish may be dusty orange, olive or rusty brown with white undersides, the inside meat is bright orange, not unlike the meat of salmon.

Based on the reliable Woolly Bugger blueprint, and the accepted fact that smallmouth adore rubber legs, the Already Crunched Crawdad incorporates white and fluorescent orange to simulate the shredded meat of a wounded crayfish. I believe the white and bright orange rubber legs are strike triggers for smallmouth, further enhanced by the marabou tail. Even when bass don't see other bass crunching crawdads, this fly produces strikes, particularly when dead-drifted. In murky water, the Already Crunched Crawdad is easier to see with all-orange legs, and it's reasonable to assume that the bass can see it more easily, too.

Not long after I started using this fly in the summer of '98, I gave guide Mike Morris a copy. On his next trip, his client caught 32 smallmouth ranging from eight to 15 inches before the fly finally fell apart. Most importantly, smallmouth approve the Already Crunched Crawdad.

Already Crunched Crawdad
(Deke Meyer)

Hook: 2x or 3x-long hook, standard or heavy wire, sizes 6 to 10

Thread: Brown 3/0

Weight: Lead or non-toxic wire (10 to 15 turns)

Tail: Tuft of white marabou next to tuft of fluorescent orange marabou

Butt: Fluorescent orange flash chenille (Glo-Brite, Crystal Chenille, etc.)

Body: Brown flash chenille (Glo-Brite, Crystal Chenille, etc.)

Legs: Medium round rubber, fluorescent orange, and white

Head: Optional, medium gold bead

Notes: Other options include an all-orange body;

all-orange legs; varying overall weight for different sink rates by varying number of wraps and size of lead or non-toxic wire, or adding lead or non-toxic barbell-type eyes.

Branham's Crayfish
(Joe Branham)

Hook: Tiemco 8089, size 10

Thread: 6/0 burnt orange

Tail: Continuation of burnt orange bucktail (over hook eye)

Weight: Small lead barbell eyes

Body: Burnt orange chenille

Shellback: Burnt orange bucktail; Liquid Rubber

Legs: Burnt orange palmered grizzly hackle

Mouthparts: Burnt orange bucktail; pearl Krystal Flash

Claws: Burnt orange grizzly hackle tips

Antennae: 2 strands black Krystal Flash

Eyes: Sewing pins painted black or burnt mono

Weedguard: Mason hard mono 15-pound, two single strands

Notes: When on the lake or river bottom, the Branham

Crayfish does not sit flat, as you would view it in the vise. Instead, the fly is propped up on a tripod consisting of the tail and the two weedguard mono strands, which puts the hook point up away from the bottom, and the front claws up in a defensive posture. Available from Umpqua Feather Merchants (wholesale).

Burk's Hot Claw Crayfish
(Andy Burk)

Hook: Tiemco 5263, size 2 to 8

Antennae: Silicone strands

Claws: Vernille; marabou

Eyes: Black mono barbell, small

Legs: Silicone strands

Body: Dubbing, coarse with sparkle added

Weighted Eyes: Extra-large non-toxic, colored with permanent marker, 5-minute Epoxy, extra-fine pearlescent glitter

Weedguard: Mason hard monofilament, 15# for size 10, 20# for size 6, 25# for size 2

Notes: The olive version has hot chartreuse marabou.

I can't imagine stuffing a whole crayfish in my mouth and happily crunching down on claws, carapace, legs, antennae and all, but bass don't seem to mind. In fact, they relish gobbling crawdads whenever they get the chance.

Zooming in on this piscatorial preference, Andy Burk of Reno, Nevada has designed a crayfish pattern with some innovative features. He noticed that his gear-slinging compadres on Shasta Lake were doing well with crawdad lures decked out in a rusty-brown coloration with bright orange claws—a concept light years removed from the standard, somber-toned crayfish fly.

So Andy deviated from the norm by installing a strike-attracting, attention-getter in the form of tufts of fluorescent marabou on stalks to simulate claws. Andy uses vernille for the claw stems because vernille is stiff enough to allow tying on of the marabou, yet will flex when you retrieve the fly along the lake bottom or in river current. Also, the stiffness of the vernille helps the fly track point-up when fished. The epoxy-covered weighted eyes help flip the fly over, and they resemble the tail fan of a crayfish.

Andy says, "My number-one tactic is to go nice and slow. I like to cast it towards steep, rocky banks, where I can crawl it down. I use a fast-sink line, leader length about six feet. Normally, I'll start out with a real slow retrieve, just crawling it along the bottom. On Lake Shasta, in the spring, the bass are seeing a lot of crayfish coming out of their burrows, starting to get active again. The bass swim right over and pick up the fly, so you get the harder grabs."

Andy also employs a panic retrieve. He'll cast the fly towards the bank, and allow the line and fly to settle. He crawls the fly a ways, then gives it fast, short jerks, until he's covered two or three feet of bottom very quickly. When Andy finds early morning bass in shallow water along the bank, he'll let the fly plop down, then immediately execute a fast-strip retrieve.

"This last fall, I was fishing a floating line, a 14-foot leader, and I was just casting to rocky areas. I would move the fly a couple of times real quick, let it settle, move it a couple of times real quick, and let it settle. The line would just draw under, just like you would see when a trout takes a little *Callibaetis* nymph. You had to set up really hard and really fast."

Besides tricking various species of bass, the Hot Claw Crayfish also deceives trout. Andy says, "One of my friends caught a real nice six-pound brown on the McCloud River this last fall on a size-four rusty-orange Hot Claw."

Since crayfish can live several years, they are found on the piscatorial menu year round. Put a little salsa on the banquet table and a zing in your reel with a Burk's Hot Claw. Available from The Fly Shop and wholesale from Umpqua Feather Merchants.

Clouser's Crayfish
(Bob Clouser)

Hook: Tiemco 5263, sizes 6 to 10
Claws: Mallard flank dyed olive green
Antennae: Pheasant tail fibers
Body: Front, gray Antron; abdomen, orange Antron
Legs: Palmered pale variant hackle
Carapace: Furry foam, olive green
Tail: Furry foam, olive green
Weight: Lead wire under body
Notes: Bob Clouser tied this olive green version; others are tan turkey and dark brown turkey. Available from Clouser's Fly Shop and wholesale from Umpqua Feather Merchants (see Sources, page 130).

Dave's Craw
(Dave Rabe)

Hook: 3x-long streamer, bent, size 1/0
Antennae: Brown mono (20-pound Maxima chameleon)
Pincers: Red fox squirrel tail
Body: Palmered natural rabbit Zonker strip, trimmed
Legs: The above, not trimmed
Carapace: Chamois
Rib: Copper wire
Tail: Same as carapace
Eyes: Lead or non-toxic barbell

Dave's Mini-Craw
(Dave Rabe

Hook: 3x-long streamer, sizes 2 to 6
Antennae: Small round black rubber strands
Pincers: Red fox squirrel tail
Body: Dubbing, light olive
Legs: Small round black rubber strands
Carapace: Chamois
Rib: Copper wire
Tail: Same as carapace
Eyes: Black mono
Notes: Dave says, "A short, quick twitch or a deep, slow crawl works best. This small crayfish has provided a large number of fish in the middle of summer."

Dyer's Mr. Mud Bug
(John Dyer)

Hook: Tiemco 200BR, size 4
Antennae: Sili Legs, one pair each, orange, brown
Claws: Rabbit fur from underbody, glued at base to form claw "stems"
Body: 9/16-inch x 3-inch Furry Foam, olive or brown
Underbody: Palmered rabbit strip, orange
Legs & Gills: Trimmed rabbit from underbody
Tail: Furry Foam
Notes: Crayfish markings on body with black and orange permanent markers. John says, "The main theme is to simulate the body profile and position of a small craw-dad. The tail is tucked under to represent a swimming

crawdad." Furry Foam is available at some fly shops, or at craft or fabric stores as a blanket material, and you can dye it.

Henry's Crawfish
(Henry Williamson)

Hook: 2x- or 3x-long shank, heavy wire, sizes 4-10
Tail: Natural deer hair
Hackle: Optional, brown
Body: Natural deer hair
Eyes: Lead barbell, or other weighted eyes
Weedguard: Optional
Notes: I was introduced to this fly by Chip Hall when I was fishing with him at Gillionville Plantation, Albany, Georgia. Chip's version was a take-off of a bonefish fly by Tim Borski of Islamorada, Florida, but this final crawfish is a simplified rendition by Henry Williamson. Henry is a fly-fishing instructor from northern Georgia with an eye towards designing flies that are easy to tie and catch fish.

This crayfish pattern is simple, but deadly for largemouth and smallmouth bass, and for any fish that eat crayfish. The mottled effect of natural deer hair mimics the broken camouflage of natural crayfish; when crayfish

swim, their claws are swept straight back behind them, as suggested by the deer-hair tail. Also, when bass bite this fly, the deer hair is kind of crunchy, just as the natural crayfish must be, so bass tend to hold onto the fly long enough for you to set the hook.

I have to agree with Chip Hall's assessment of Henry's Crawfish: "This fly is the greatest thing since grits."

Kiraw
(Richard A. Whitner & Capt. Kirby Lacour)

Hook: Ring eye, standard or long shank
Antennae: Krystal Flash or moose mane
Eyes: Melted mono, painted black
Legs: Pheasant rump, saddle, schlappen or waterfowl feathers, deer hair, synthetic hair, sparkle material
Body: Flexo tubing cut at an angle, opened up; edge coated with Softex; colored with permanent marker or EZ-Shape Sparkle Body
Tail: Extension of top half of Flexo tubing
Claws: Feathers, glued or foam
Weight: Lead barbell on rear of hook shank near bend
Notes: Fly co-designed by Richard Whitner of the Sporting Life Orvis shop in New Orleans and Captain

Kirby Lacour of BKD Guide Service of Kenner, Louisiana.

Crayfish

Likakis's Two-Minute Crawdad
(John Likakis)

Hook: Eagle Claw 3214 Aberdeen, size 1 or 1/0
Claws: Two splayed furnace hackles
Body: Chenille stems, brown or orange
Legs: Saddle hackle palmered through first third of body
Notes: John Likakis, editor of *Warmwater Fly Fishing* magazine, says, "The Two-Minute Crawdad meets all my criteria for a fly: easy to tie, cheap, and catches plenty of fish. The body is made from chenille stem, which is essentially big pipe cleaner available at craft stores. The wire core of the chenille stem provides all the weight needed, and assures that the crawdad sinks in a level attitude."

Lynch's B'wana's Craw
(Dan Lynch)

Hook: Gamakatsu round-bend worm hook, size 3/0 and 1/0
Weight: Lead barbell eyes (small for 3/0, extra small for 1/0)
Antennae: Rubber or Sili Legs
Rattle: 3 or 4mm glass
Legs: Rubber or Sili Legs
Body: Chenille or yarn
Overbody: Ultra suede; epoxy over body, not claws; optional extra-fine pearlescent glitter or sparkle fingernail polish
Weedguard: Strands of stiff mono (4 strands for 3/0 and 1/0)
Notes: This is an earlier 5/0 version with bucktail for antennae. Natural crayfish exhibit wide variation in colors, including black, olive, brown, tan, rust and orangish red. You can tie your Craw to match natural coloration, or as an attractor, such as in navy blue. Generally, the body will be a lighter tone than the carapace (which darkens when epoxied), but body color is not crucial.

Dan Lynch of Ennis, Texas, guides on Lake Fork. He says, "I believe that about 40% of a bass's diet is crawfish. You can catch quite a number of fish on my fly and it won't fall apart. With some of my crawfish flies I've caught 50 fish on them, and they still look the same. They just have scars on them, and to fix them back up, just run some more epoxy over the top of them and they're brand new again.

"I started tying flies when I was a teenager, and I've got 35 years of experience. A lot of my flies aren't real pretty, but they work. That's what my deal is."

Of course, a prime objective for bass is designing a fly that will defeat snags, but still catch fish. Dan's weed guard is effective because the monofilament strands are locked in the upright position by epoxy, remaining stiff enough to prevent the fly from snagging, yet they collapse when bass bite.

Dan says, "When bass hit the fly, they don't feel the weed guard because all crawfish have stickers sticking out of them. And perch, and anything else they feed on, have spines. Bass don't care; they're made for that—that's what they eat. A four-pound bass can take the biggest crawfish ever grown and crush him flat in one bite.

"If you want to see how tough bass are, take one of those big tiger salamanders that we use—and their skin is like leather—and let a bass bite it three or four times. Then bring it back; it will be all ripped up—and you can't even rip that hide with your fingers. And yet bass can do it with their mouth.

"Some of these six-, seven-pound bass will take a perch bigger than the size of your hand, crunch the perch one time, and three-fourths of the scales are gone

Hot Bass Flies

off the perch. They do it because it makes them easier to digest. It's the same with shad or shiners or whatever they're feeding on—the scales are some of the hard stuff they don't have to digest. When bass hit them, you'll see scales going everywhere, from out of the back of the bass's gills. You just don't realize how strong bass are."

Dan's favorite retrieve is a short pull on the line to get the B'wana's Craw to lift up off the bottom, then a pause to let it drift back down. While it's true that a frightened crayfish will scoot along, crayfish often pop up just a ways off the bottom to look around, then drift back down again. Dan finds that mimicking this behavior is deadly.

The B'wana's Craw in size 6 is lethal for smallmouth, and trout love this bit of crustacean candy. While fishing the San Juan River in New Mexico, Dan observed that most fly-flingers were catching 15-inch trout by matching the midge hatch. He was soon circled by a ring of curious fishermen after he landed yet another jumbo trout over three pounds on his B'wana's Craw, size 1/0. And although he didn't have the onlookers when he fished the White River in Arkansas, he found those big browns love the B'wana's Craw, too. For more information, contact Dan Lynch (see Sources, page 130).

Mercer's Poxybou Rattle Craw
(Mike Mercer)

Hook: Tiemco 200, size 4
Tail: Mottled turkey
Body: Dubbing, rust brown; orange thread rib; rattle
Carapace: Mottle turkey; epoxy
Legs: Hen back feather fibers
Claws: Orangish-brown marabou
Antennae: Pumpkin silicone strands
Head: Dubbing
Eyes: Black mono
Weight: Lead barbell
Notes: Available from The Fly Shop (see Sources).

Robinson's Mud Bug
(Joe Robinson)

Hook: Tiemco 7999 Salmon/Steelhead, size 2
Weight: Lead barbell eyes, flattened, under tail
Antennae: Orange silicone strands
Claws: Ultra suede; permanent marker
Legs: Orange silicone strands
Body: Orange Antron over foam
Overbody: Ultra suede; permanent marker; abdomen ribbed with copper wire
Tail: Ultra suede; permanent marker
Weedguard: Loop of stiff mono
Notes: This is the orange version; the other is dark brown.

Crayfish

Sanchez Madam X Crawdad
(Scott Sanchez)

Hook: Dai-Riki 270 natural bend; Tiemco 200R, sizes 4 to 10

Thread: 3/0 orange

Weight: Lead wire under bullet head

Abdomen: Natural elk hair tied bullet-head style over front half of hook

Thorax: The tips of the abdomen; trim flat on bottom of the fly

Legs: Tan Super Floss or thin rubber

Antennae: Tan Super Floss or thin rubber

Eyes: Black plastic bead chain

Notes: Scott Sanchez of Livingston, Montana says, "This is a Madam X that has been converted to a crawdad. The shape of a Madam X seemed like a crawfish

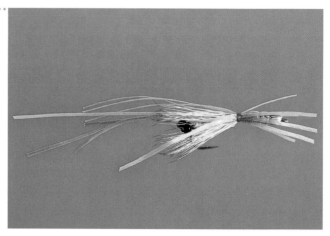

profile to me and it was a quick fly to tie. This fly has accounted for some magnum sunfish up to a foot long and has worked on tough bonefish. Try this in colors that match the crawfish in your area and the color of the stream bottom."

Skip's Dad
(Skip Morris)

Hook: 1x to 3x-long, sizes 12 to 6

Tail: Pheasant tail fibers dyed dark brown

Nose: Brown Antron dubbing

Weight: Lead or non-toxic barbell

Pincers: Pheasant tail fibers dyed dark brown

Back: Pheasant tail fibers dyed dark brown

Rib: Fine copper wire

Abdomen: Brown Antron dubbing

Notes: For the tying description for this smallmouth fly, see Skip's book, *The Art of Tying the Bass Fly.* You can sustitute natural pheasant tail fibers if brown isn't available. Available from Umpqua Feather Merchants (wholesale).

Spirit River's Bunny Crayfish
(Spirit River)

Hook: Long shank, sizes 4 and 8

Antennae: Rubber strands

Head/Thorax: Foam; Antron rust-orange dubbing

Eyes: Black mono

Claws: Rust-orange rabbit strip

Body: Antron rust-orange dubbing

Legs: SRI Emu

Carapace: Rust Bodi-Stretch

Rib: Copper wire

Tail: Continuation of carapace

Notes: This is the rust-orange version. The other is dark brown. Available wholesale from Spirit River.

Starkweather's Crayfish
(George Starkweather)

Hook: Daiichi 1730, sizes 2 to 10
Antennae: Peccary
Claws: Ultra-suede, tan, top speckled with black permanent marker; super glued to body
Carapace: Ultra-suede, tan, top lined with black permanent marker
Eyes: Burnt monofilament or black plastic dumbbell eyes
Body: Aunt Lydia's Sparkle Yarn, brown; abdomen ribbed with fine copper wire
Legs: Speckle-Flake Sili Legs, burnt orange
Weight: Lead dumbbell eyes
Tail: Ultra-suede, tan, top lined with black permanent marker
Notes: George ties this in tan, brown, or olive. He uses glycerin on the legs so they slide easily when he sews

them through the body. He says, "There are similar flies to this one; however, I have modified the fly to suit my purposes. This particular crayfish pattern is very involved and time consuming to tie. However, it is the most realistic pattern that I have been able to come up with, great for largemouth and smallmouth bass."

Whitlock's Near-Nuff Crayfish
(Dave Whitlock)

Hook: Tiemco 5263, sizes 4-8
Antennae: Two strands each: pearl Krystal Flash, silicone with painted orange tips, small black Spanflex
Claws: Hen hackle, two pair, painted orange dots
Eyes: Small black mono
Body: Rabbit-Antron Rabbit and Antron dubbing; palmered soft grizzly hackle trimmed off bottom
Nose: Rabbit fur
Tail: Rabbit fur
Weight: Lead barbell eyes painted
Notes: This is the gray version. Also in brownish orange. Available from Umpqua Feather Merchants (wholesale).

Wyatt's Hook-Up Crawfish
(Eddie Wyatt)

Hook: Tiemco 5262, size 2 or 4, bent-keel style
Antennae: Brown ostrich, glue rubbed onto ends to slim down
Mouthparts: Sixteen strands orange Krystal Flash; orange dubbing
Claws: Natural tan rabbit fur strips, notched on ends
Body: Spun natural tan rabbit fur; trimmed flat on belly, round on top
Legs: Guard hair strands not trimmed from body
Eyes: Lead barbell, medium (7/32) or large (8/32)
Notes: Eddie Wyatt of Johnson City, Tennessee also ties an all-black Hook-Up Hellgrammite (see Subsurface Flies).

Yamagata's Spun Crawdad
(Jeff Yamagata)

Hook: TMC 300 or 5263, sizes 2-8

Antennae: Silicon strands, pumpkin with orange tips; orange bucktail

Claws: Chamois; black permanent marker

Eyes: Clear 30-pound mono, burned; black permanent marker

Body: Spun McFlyfoam, orange, dark brown, tan

Legs: Silicon strands, pumpkin with orange tips

Tail: McFlyfoam, orange; brown permanent marker

Notes: Available at A-1 Fish Fly Fishing Supplies.

When fishing subsurface for bass, try different retrieves. When you fish a popper, work that bug like a puppet, experiment with any fly-antics you think will entice a strike. Likewise when fishing deep terrain, become a maestro of fly manipulation—make that bug seem alive.

Hot Bass Flies

Guide Dan Lynch uses his years of experience with conventional bass tackle and big bass on Lake Fork, Texas to develop his own fly designs.

Crayfish

Innovative fly-master Andy Burk loves to trick finny critters with his unique creatures of fur and feather.

Hot Bass Flies

Chapter 7

Subsurface Flies

A bass will most often take a subsurface fly into its mouth with a gob of water while it moves forward, this translates up the leader, fly line and to your hand as a very subtle take.

It would be wonderful if bass always lived in shallow water and gleefully attacked our poppers, or even our surface sliders and divers. But they don't. And if you want to consistently catch bass, you need to present your flies subsurface, at the depth the bass are holding.

Subsurface fishing for bass can be tough because bass come up behind the fly and suck it in with a gob of water as they keep moving. True, they inhale the fly and bite down on it, but the gob of water and the forward glide of the bass translates up the tippet, up the leader, up the fly line and finally into your hand as a gentle twitch, tug, pull or hesitation. This is difficult to detect, and you need time to react and set the hook.

When looking to trick subsurface bass, besides the obvious visual qualities of the fly's color and movement on the retrieve, some fly designers incorporate a water-pushing feature. Bass can feel when their prey displaces water by swimming, and are more likely to pounce on flies that displace water on the retrieve, that generate a kind of underwater wave. One common construction is a deer-hair head tied slider-style, such as you might find on a Muddler, but fished subsurface instead of topwater.

Barr's Bouface
(John Barr)

Hook: Tiemco Stinger 8089, size 2 and 6; Tiemco 811S, sizes 2/0 and 3/0 for five-inch flies; size 1 for three-inch flies

Tail: Chartreuse rabbit strip; black Krystal Flash; pearl Flashabou

Body: Chartreuse marabou

Head: Black thread

Weedguard: Wire loop (optional)

Notes: This is the chartreuse version. Other colors include black, red/white, yellow/black, black/blue, also a gold-bead version. Available from Umpqua Feather Merchants (wholesale).

John Barr of Boulder, Colorado says, "The Bouface was originally designed as a pike fly back in '81 or '82. I tried all kinds of different pike flies, but it ended up being my best pike fly. I've caught half a dozen pike here in Colorado over 25 pounds on the Bouface. Then I started fishing for bass, and all my big bass have been on the Bouface, as well. It's a real good, big-fish fly. And about ninety percent of the time I use either black or chartreuse. I've found if they're not going to take one of those, they're just not on the bite. I like to simplify my life and my fly patterns.

"I started with a seven-inch fly, but now tie them about five inches and about three inches. The Bouface is a real versatile pattern because I don't weight it and you can swim it real slowly along the top. It has all this built-in action—everything is breathing and quivering and moving, so you can fish it real slowly over the tops of weed beds, over roots, weeds or in open water.

"You can also fish it like a Jig-N-Pig. In the water it looks like a Jig-N-Pig and it looks just like a crawdad. I'll put a size BB or 3/0 split shot on the tippet, just in front of the fly or a sliding worm weight pegged with a toothpick. I fish it like a Jig-N-Pig when the bass are in pre-spawn, perimeter cruising, relating to the edges. I cast it into the bank and let it fall down, then just hop it back like a Jig-N-Pig. Sometimes I hop it along with my rod, other times I use a jerk-like retrieve."

Barr's Dragonfly Nymph
(John Barr)

Hook: Tiemco 5263, size 6

Tail: Black marabou

Body: Dark gray Antron

Legs: Black soft hackle

Shellback: Mylar; black permanent marker

Rib: Silver wire

Wingpads: Mylar; black permanent marker

Head: Dark gray Antron

Barr's Terminator
(John Barr)
Hook: Tiemco 8089 size 6 and 10
Tail: Black marabou; pearl Krystal Flash
Body: Black Estaz; palmered grizzly hackle
Legs: White rubber
Head: Large brass bead

Barry's Pike Fly
(Barry Reynolds)
Hook: TMC 811S, sizes 1/0-3/0
Thread: Flat waxed 3/0
Tail: Krystal Flash; rabbit strip
Collar: Palmered rabbit fur strip
Head: Epoxy over thread
Eyes: Prismatic
Colors: Chartreuse, black, red/white, red/yellow, pink, white
Notes: Barry Reynolds of Aurora, Colorado says, "Basically, it's just a variation of the Alaskan Flesh Fly. We were using it for big rainbows on the Alagnak River in Alaska. With the movement of the fly, we thought if we tried bigger sizes and more pike-enticing colors, that the pike would react well to it. It's our number-one pike

fly and its durability is phenomenal—twenty or thirty fish for each fly without its being chewed to death." Available commercially at fly shops (wholesale from Umpqua Feather Merchants).

Bendback
Hook: Bendback Mustad 34005; Tiemco 411S; can bend other hooks into Bendback shape; varied sizes
Tail: Optional, usually not included
Hackle: Optional, varied colors
Gills: Optional, red thread, chenille or Flashabou
Wing: Bucktail or synthetics; Krystal Flash or Flashabou; optional grizzly hackle, peacock herl topping
Body: Tubular Mylar, braided poly flash or Crystal Chenille
Eyes: Optional, painted or adhesive
Notes: Tied by Mike Huffman of Dallas, Texas. You can add lead wire on the low point on the shank to further hook-point-up effect; some tiers enclose a rattle in the body; numerous color variations.

Blanton's Whistler
(Dan Blanton)

Hook: Short shank: Mustad 9175; Eagle Claw 254 Sea Guard; Tiemco 800S; sizes 2/0 to 4/0

Thread: Red Danville flat waxed

Tail: Bucktail; Silver Flashabou, 25 to 30 strands; multi-colored Crystal Flash, 15 to 20 strands each side; most have grizzly hackle flanks

Hackle: Three saddle hackles (large and webby)

Body: .030 lead wire (2 amp), 8 to 10 turns; chenille, medium red, 2 turns only

Eyes: Silver bead chain, large

Notes: This is the Sunset Flashtail Whistler. There are over 20 color variations. After 30 years the Whistler design has proven deadly on any fish that feeds on other fish, including bass. Available from Umpqua Feather Merchants (wholesale).

Dan Blanton of San Jose, California says, "The Whistler was created to compete with the lead-head, bucktail jig, one of history's top producing artificials. The secret to its huge success is in its action, the dipping, diving motion that mocks the antics of an injured baitfish—an action that almost instantly pushes a predator's strike buttons. The Whistler has a built-in action that is identical to that of a jig. A bucktail jig gets its action from the mass of lead located at the eye of the hook. This forward heft is what causes the dipping-and-diving action during the retrieve. The Whistler is tied as a weighted fly, concentrating the weight forward in order to achieve the same effect."

BossBob's Glo-Bug Streamer
(Bob Long, Jr.)

Hook: Mustad 3366, size 1 or 1/0

Top: Full tuft of marabou, grizzly marabou or fox fur

Belly: Full tuft of marabou, grizzly marabou or fox fur

Body: Four saddle hackles, two facing in on each side

Flash: Krystal Flash or Fire Fly along each side

Head: Glo-Bug yarn or lamb's wool stacked and clipped to shape

Eyes: Doll eyes or Witchcraft 3D eyes to match species imitated

Weedguard: 30-pound hard Mason or Climax

Notes: This is the baby bullhead, with brown hen hackle, brown marabou, brown wool and solid plastic eyes, black on orange. Bob Long, Jr. of Chicago, also matches the round goby, alewife, smelt, sculpins, darters, madtoms, and other prey fish.

BossBob's Rabbit-Strip Leech
(Bob Long, Jr.)

Hook: Tiemco 200; Mustad 80050; Dai-Riki 1270, 270; size 4

Tail: Rabbit strip, hide side up (1.5 to 2 times body length)

Body: Vernille

Flash: 4 strands Fire Fly Tye each side of rabbit strip

Rib: 4 strands Fire Fly

Hackle: Wide, soft, saddle hackle or schlappen palmered along body

Eyes: Umpqua 7/32 or 8/32-ounce lead barbells, black pupil on red, permanent marker or adhesive eyes

Weedguard: 30-pound hard Mason or Climax

Notes: This is the burnt orange version. Bob ties others, such as black, chartreuse, rusty brown, wine, yellow. A jazz disc jockey in Chicago for many years, Bob says, "While most tiers seem more impressed with the Glo-Bug head streamers, this is one of the most effective flies I've ever used. It's replaced Woolly Buggers, Woolly Worms, or Woolly whatever's in my arsenal. In addition to largemouth, it takes bluegill, crappie, rock bass, small-mouth, white bass, stripers, perch, walleye, sauger, steelies, browns, salmon, suckers, carp and channel cats (two of them).

"This is the fly I give to kids when I'm introducing them to the fly rod. It's difficult, if not impossible, to fish wrong and it takes a variety of species so it keeps things interesting for the youngsters (and me, too).

"This is a great fly for dropping into pockets of

vegetation, jigging along the edges of weed beds, swimming over weed tops and other structure, vertical jigging next to timber, crawling along gravely/rocky bottoms, swimming just under the surface, or hopping stop-and-go."

In true DJ style, Bob says, "Just a fly that evolved and has become quite an effective fly for me. Alright, I mean a really effective fly for me. OK! It's one hot mother for ya! Look! Under the water! It's a leech, it's a crayfish, it's a hellgrammite, it's a minnow—it's an all-around, all-purpose, impressionistic/attractor pattern!"

His BossBob's Leech TNG (The Next Generation) is tied on a Partridge CS/10 size 1/o hook and has two rabbit-strip tails, hide-to-hide, tied in wine, black, yellow, burnt orange, white, rusty brown. He says, "It's bulkier and chewy and is tough to cast when wet, but is light and fluid once in the water. So it calls for lead wraps in addition to the lead eyes (and I often need split shot to boot) for big waters and bigger fish."

Bradham's Rubber Hackled Bumble Bug
(Bramblett Bradham)

Hook: Stinger, size 2

Weight: Lead wire

Body: Chenille, woven black and chartreuse

Legs: Yellow round rubber as a collar

Head: Black chenille

Eyes: Non-toxic, black on white; optionally, weighted eyes

Notes: Bramblett Bradham of Charleston, South Carolina, says, "I strip it along the edges of the bank, with short, choppy strips—those rubber legs have a really good action to them. It's a strange kind of fly, but a lot of times fish will take it and hold it in their mouth and kind of swim along at the same speed. You'll feel a

slight tug and you'll have to set real hard, but it's caught a lot of fish."

Burk's Aggravator
(Andy Burk)

Hook: Tiemco 200, sizes 4-12
Tag: Pearlescent Krystal Flash
Tail: Tannish-olive marabou
Underbody: Non-toxic wire, medium .020
Body: Hare's mask dubbing
Legs: Silicone, pumpkin with black speckles
Wingcase: Dark turkey tail feather
Collar: Extra-dark hare's mask dubbing
Head: Gold, copper or brass bead
Notes: Collar can be black rabbit fur dubbing or peacock herl; other color variations include black, olive and prince. Available from Umpqua Feather Merchants (wholesale).

In his article in *California Fly Fisher*, January 1996, Andy Burk of Reno, Nevada says, "Sometimes you just have to show fish something different, something they've never seen before. Sometimes you have to show fish something that flat aggravates them. A fly so bizarre, so irritating, that they don't merely want to eat it—they want to kill it.

"Enter the Aggravator Nymph. The Aggravator was created after a long, hot, frustrating August day on the lower reaches of the upper Sacramento River. My fishing partner Dave Ramirez and I had been fishing this water for spotted bass and smallmouth bass that had migrated from the too-warm waters of Lake Shasta, and we had been terrorizing them on a regular basis for about three weeks. The fish were finally wising up to our fast-stripped minnow imitations and surface poppers; catch rates had plummeted, with the areas that previously had produced dozens of feisty bass now yielding only one or two half-hearted tugs.

"Clearly, the bass had become so conditioned to seeing our usual patterns and retrieves that they began ignoring them altogether. We knew the fish were still holding in their usual haunts—we could see them!

"Dave was the first to crack. To hell with 'em! he shouted in exasperation. I'm gonna put on a nymph and catch some trout!

"About five bass later I began to suspect Dave was onto something, although maybe not exactly what he had intended. I frantically searched my vest, but all my nymph boxes were back at the car. Should I swallow my pride and ask Dave for a few nymphs? No way!

"But to my chagrin, dead-drifting streamers and large Woolly Buggers couldn't cut it. By the time night fell I hadn't had a single tap.

"On our walk to the car, Dave was still on his fly-fisher's high, having, so to speak, conquered. Lucky me. I pried carefully for information, and Dave eagerly gave it. He showed me a ratty-looking Golden Stonefly nymph, one that had obviously been chewed on by a lot of bass. The fly had taken a number of nice fish on the dead-drift, but had caught many more when twitched slightly every now and then as it bounced along the bottom.

"Later, at my vise, I thought of all the things that might cause a bass to eat a nymph. I began pulling out bags of different materials: marabou for the fluttery motion it provides; Krystal Flash for twinkling highlights; rubber legs to enhance an appearance of life; hare's mask dubbing, with its nicely mottled buggy look; turkey tail for a darkly-mottled wing case; and a large gold bead to give the fly a seductive up-down jig on the retrieve.

"I assembled the various components onto a hook, then swam the completed fly through the test tank I keep at my fly-tying bench. The bass will not be able to leave this pattern alone, I thought to myself.

"And they couldn't. On our next visit to the upper Sac, Dave again fished his Golden Stone nymph, and I fished my new pattern. It caught rainbows—big rainbows. It caught bass—big bass. The new design had worked; I was one happy camper.

"I've been tying the Aggravator in a variety of colors and sizes, and fishing it either dead-drifted under an indicator or, if on stillwaters, stripped slowly on a deeply sunken line. The fly seems to work just about everywhere I take it. I've actually seen several fish that had displayed indifference to any number of flies and presentations pounce on the Aggravator as though it were a mortal enemy. Bass, trout, panfish, steelhead and even a salmon have fallen prey to this strange-looking fly.

"Give it a try (and try other colors, like black and olive); you'll be Aggravating fish in no time at all."

Burk's Flat Tail Worm
(Andy Burk)

Hook: Tiemco 8089 Stinger, size 10
Tail: Purple badger hackle; purple marabou; Krystal Flash, red, purple; chartreuse marabou
Body: Purple Crystal Chenille; palmered black hackle
Head: Black dubbing
Eyes: Lead barbell painted black on red
Weedguard: Mason hard mono 20-pound
Notes: This is the purple version. The other color is root beer. Available from The Fly Shop.

Burk's Hot Flash Minnow
(Andy Burk)

Hook: TMC 811S, sizes 2 to 6; TMC 8089, sizes 2 to 10
Thread: White 3/0, Danville Flymaster Plus
Tail: Polar Bear Super Hair or Ultra Hair; pearl Angel Hair
Body: Angel Hair, pearl green, silver, chartreuse, olive
Eyes: Silver holographic, black on silver; epoxy
Notes: This is the shad version; the other is golden shiner. Andy Burk of Reno, Nevada says, "I use Hot Flash Minnows in several different ways, all of which have produced well for me at one time or another. As with any such imitation, the fly and its presentation must take into account three triggering factors that induce attack, and these basic triggers remain the same regardless of where and how such a fly is used. These factors are size, motion, and color. Generally, color seems to be less critical than size and motion.

"Most anglers underestimate the importance of a streamer's size. Usually, all the baitfish in a school are about the same length. In the lakes I fish, I rarely see any five-inch threadfin shad mixed with a school of two- or three-inch specimens. Predators become accustomed to feeding selectively on minnows of a given size, so I always try to match the size of the predominant prey. If you find yourself on the water with three-inch flies when you want smaller ones, you can snip the Hot Flash Minnow down as desired.

"How the fly behaves in the water is just as important as its size. Most baitfish are nervous, twitchy creatures that panic easily—an instinct necessary for survival of the species even though that same instinct may be fatal to individual minnows. Toss a pebble into a concentration of minnows, and the school will erupt and then ball up again quickly after the disturbance has subsided.

"Quite often, predators exploit this tendency by attacking or ambushing in packs. They slash through the minnow school, battering the bait and rapidly opening and closing their mouths. This cripples some of the minnows and disorients many that aren't injured. Then the predators move through the school again, gobbling the disabled. Disoriented minnows that have broken away from the school dart about aimlessly for a brief time—but long enough for some of them to be easy pickings.

"If you toss your streamer into this kind of melee and strip it back rapidly, the odds are that nothing will happen. Your fly is imitating a minnow that is neither injured nor disoriented, and will be ignored by predators. On the other hand, suppose your sparkling, attention-getting streamer imitates a slow-sinking, stunned or injured minnow that can't get away quickly. That's the kind that gets gulped. To achieve this illusion, cast and then keep a tight line as the fly sinks.

"You won't get the desired response every time, of course. When you don't, then you can retrieve the fly with very short, erratic motions interspersed with long pauses between strips. This makes the fly behave like a disoriented minnow attempting to escape but moving aimlessly.

"You'll probably spend a lot more time prospecting in water where nothing seems to be happening, searching for aggressive fish that will lunge at any minnow that comes along. For such prospecting, I cast the fly far out, let it sink, then use a rip retrieve—fast, long strips to swim the streamer back in a natural (nervous but unmolested) way. The idea is to cover as much water as possible while maintaining a realistic deception.

"Prospecting can be tiring since it demands a lot of casting and retrieving. To make it still tougher, the fast, long strips are apt to get a lot of short strikes and misses. Cast again, retrieving more slowly and seductively.

"I regularly carry two rods, rigged with identically but with Hot Flash Minnows of two different colors. If I miss a fish while retrieving my first-choice fly and it won't come back for a second pass, I throw the second Hot Flash Minnow and quite often catch the fish.

"I carry Hot Flash Minnows in a wide array of colors to match the prevalent bait by using synthetics that emphasize their general overall color. Look closely at the iridescent sides of a threadfin shad, for instance, and you'll notice highlights of pink, blue, violet, silver, green and yellow. Fortunately, the dominant reflection will be silver, whereas gold dominates when you examine a chub. Habitat can change the dominant color—I know some areas where silvery minnows are dull yellow. I carry Hot Flash Minnows in various colors but count chiefly on flies tied mostly silver or mostly gold. My fly boxes always contain a few versions that feature attractor colors like red and chartreuse—unrealistic but often effective, especially when I'm trying to locate bass." Available from The Fly Shop and wholesale from Umpqua Feather Merchants (shad and golden shiner).

Burk's Rattlin' Spider JigFly
(Andy Burk)

Hook: Stinger, sizes 2
Tail: Rabbit strip
Collar: Chenille, medium
Legs: Silicone; Accent Flash
Body: Mylar braid over rattle
Eyes: Large non-toxic eyes, colored with permanent
marker; 5-minute epoxy; extra-fine pearlescent glitter
Weedguard: Single strand .018 wire, bent
Notes: Colors include black, pumpkin with chartreuse tail, crayfish orange, brown with black tail, purple with black tail. Available from The Fly Shop, see Sources.

Burk's Terrible Tentacles
(Andy Burk)

Hook: Stinger, sizes 2-10
Weight: Non-toxic wire, .015 inch diameter
Tail: Silicone strands
Body: Crystal Chenille, large
Collar: Icelandic wool
Weedguard: Single strand .018 wire, bent
Notes: Colors include pearl, pearl with hot-orange-tip silicone tail, chartreuse, purple, olive; all of which Andy will pitch on floating and sinking lines, covering all depths of water. In his article "Sink the Fly Slowly" in *Warmwater Fly Fishing*, September 1997, Andy wrote: "Few bass can resist a slow-sinking, wiggly critter that

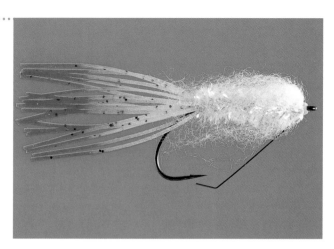

descends into their realm. When a bass is in an inactive or moderately active state, I have found that extremely slow-moving or slow-sinking imitations are far more effective than fast-moving ones. In fact, in many situations where bass are feeding actively, a slow-sinking fly will work as well as, or better than any other fly. Yet I have found very few anglers who fish slow-sinking flies regularly, and even fewer anglers who fish them effectively.

"Most of us have, at one time or another, fished a slow-sinking fly and caught fish, though the hookup might have been more by accident than design. It usually happens as you're waiting for your fly to sink and suddenly the line pulls tight and you've got a fish on. This sort of thing is a vivid reminder that we're fishing the second the fly hits the water.

"Keeping a tight line is very important when fishing with slow-sinking flies. Often the hit to a slow-sinking fly draws is very subtle. Even the largest bass can inhale a fly and reject it without giving a clue what has happened. I often wonder how many fish actually pick up and taste our flies, and then reject them without us feeling even the slightest tap.

"Slow-sinking flies come into their own when fishing for bass that are not actively pursuing baitfish, such as during the pre-spawn and immediate post-spawn times. Slow-sinking-fly tactics are great for suspended fish, too, especially during the dog days of summer.

"When fishing slow-sinking flies, almost all the action comes when the fly is sinking. After making a cast, I'll immediately make a few strips to straighten the line and leader. This also ensures that the fly straightens out and swims properly as it descends. I then focus all my attention on the tip of the fly line, watching for the subtle telltale twitch of the fish's take.

"If I see the line do anything unusual, I strike immediately. I figure that because I'm seeing the take telegraphed up the leader to the line, I'll be striking a little late most of the time. Remember, it doesn't cost anything to strike. You'll be amazed at how many of those things that you thing are nothing turn out to be bass. The best way to strike is to make a long, hard strip with your line hand until you feel the fish's weight, then sweep the rod tip to steer the fish away from any nearby cover.

"Sometimes it takes a little extra persuasion to get the fish to strike. My favorite method is one I call the dart-and-drop retrieve. Once the fly has reached the proper depth, give the line a sharp strip. This moves the fly forward one to three feet. Then let the fly sink again. The fly looks and acts like an injured baitfish, darting forward and then losing control and descending slowly. Few bass can resist this action. This technique works well with both floating and sinking lines, but I find it most effective with a sinking line. With the sinking line, strip the fly forward and then stop with the rod tip pointed down the sunken line. Don't allow any line to sag off the rod tip. The strike is very distinct: it feels like the line slowly becomes heavier, or it may just become tight in your hand. Set the hook by stripping hard with your line hand once you feel the weight of the fish.

"The real key is being aware of what is happening with your line and fly. I often take a few minutes to watch how my fly sinks and the way it looks to the fish, and how I want to make it behave under water."

Burk's V-Worm
(Andy Burk)

Hook: Stinger, size 10 (Tiemco 8089NP)
Weight: Non-toxic wire, .015-inch diameter
Tail: Vernille with marabou tip
Body: Dubbing, shaggy; optional sparkle material added
Weedguard: Mason hard monofilament, 15-pound
Notes: Colors include olive, rust, purple, black, all with hot chartreuse tip. Available from The Fly Shop and wholesale from Umpqua Feather Merchants. Andy also likes chartreuse and white, and sometimes adds specks and stripes with a waterproof pen, and blends Lite Brite or Flashabou into the dubbing.

In his article in *California Fly Fisher*, March, 1996, Andy said, "Ah, the worm turns. Conventional anglers have long snickered at us fly fishers. They, after all, had

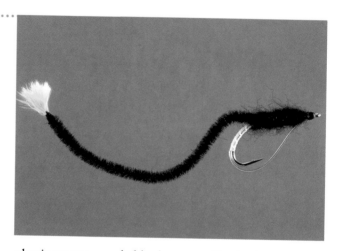

plastic worms—probably the most effective lure ever developed for largemouth bass. Plastic worms not only out-produce fly-rod-delivered bugs, they often out-produce such traditional bass lures as crankbaits and top-water plugs.

"As with many successful patterns, the V-Worm was born of necessity. I'd been doing a lot of bass fishing last year, and not surprisingly, leaving quite a few Flat-Tails stuck on the rocks and ledges of Shasta and Whiskeytown lakes. As much as I enjoy tying flies, I was having trouble keeping up with the losses—an average outing would eat up a dozen or more Flat-Tails, and I was down to a few oddball experiments tied in colors like yellow and hot pink. I needed flies, and I needed 'em quick!

"The solution to my problem came in the form of a gift from Oakland fly-tier Jeff Yamagata. He had sent me some patterns for which he had used a rotary vise to spin together strands of Vernille and Crystal Chenille, forming a long, flexible, worm-like body. (See Yamagata's Eliminator Worm.) It was a pretty cool idea, and I liked the effect, but having no rotary vise I was taking forever to spin the materials manually.

"I could skip the spin, I realized, by using medium-diameter Vernille (or Ultra Chenille). I clamped a strand in the vise, added a tail of fluorescent marabou, then attached the thing to a lightly weighted hook and dubbed a thin body. Voila! The V-Worm was created in a tad more than two minutes.

"Best of all, the largemouth loved it. When my fishing partner Sandy and I experimented with the V-Worm at Coffee Cup Lake, it seemed as if all we had to do was get the fly to the water and there would be a big bass waiting to engulf it. We even caught the same fish several times by changing the color of the worm, and Sandy capped the day with a six-plus-pounder. Not bad for a simple pattern!

"Because the V-Worm is quick and easy to tie, you needn't worry about losing them when fishing structure. In fact, I've dramatically increased my catch rates because I'm now throwing the V-Worm to places I otherwise would have skipped when I was concerned about losing flies that required ten minutes at the vise.

"The V-Worm is also versatile in its fishability. You can drag it along the bottom with a sinking line, strip it through cover like a leech, even work it on the surface. Sometimes the best retrieve is no retrieve at all."

Clouser's Minnow
(Bob Clouser)

Hook: Standard or x-long, varied sizes

Thread: White

Tail: Forms lower wing and belly, white bucktail

Wing: Rainbow Krystal Flash extended to the rear; chartreuse bucktail

Body: Tying thread over bucktail

Eyes: Weighted: lead, plated, painted or non-toxic, attached at forward third of hook shank, on top

Notes: This fly tied by Bob Clouser in March, 1998, is a copy of one of the original versions of probably the most important, and simple patterns simulating a small fish. First developed in the mid-1980's, there are now countless variations that take predator fish all over the world, including all species of bass. Many versions use synthetic materials; some tiers eliminate tying down the wing and tail materials behind the eye and simply tie down both in front of the eye.

Bob told me, "The original Clouser Minnow was designed for the darting motion of baitfish trying to escape a predator. It gives the look of a baitfish and it's sparsely dressed. The darting motion comes from the

stripping, or the motion you give the fly after the cast is done.

"When you stop your retrieve, the Minnow will drop off its plane and head towards the bottom. From either side—it doesn't necessarily drop straight down—it gets off plane and slides off to the side—mimicking that downward movement of a baitfish trying to hide. The lead eyes make the fly dip and dart with an action and speed similar to a live baitfish fleeing from a predator."

Available from Umpqua Feather Merchants (wholesale) and most fly shops, including Clouser's (see Sources, page 130).

Clouser's Baby Smallmouth
(Bob Clouser)

Hook: Tiemco 811S or Mustad 34007, sizes 1/0 and 2
Thread: Dark brown or black 3/0
Tail: White bucktail
Belly: White bucktail
Wing: Green bucktail, gold Krystal Flash; bronze Flashabou
Eyes: Metallic
Notes: Bob Clouser of Middletown, Pennsylvania says, "I designed the fly to fish the Susquehanna River in Pennsylvania for smallmouth from June through October, depending on temperature changes. It's a Clouser Minnow with a color combination to look similar to the young smallmouth bass. That color

combination is also deadly on saltwater fish such as snook and redfish." Available commercially at fly shops (wholesale from Umpqua Feather Merchants).

D's Baby Bluegill
(Darrel Sickmon)

Hook: Long shank, size 6
Tail: Olive grizzly marabou
Body: Mylar pearlescent tubing
Belly: SLF (Synthetic Living Fiber) white, yellow, gold, orange
Wing: SLF olive, black
Cheeks: SLF olive (pectoral fins)
Gills: SLF, red
Head: Permanent marker over white thread, dark olive, orange: epoxy, glitter
Eyes: Adhesive, black on gold
Notes: This is the Baby Bluegill version of D's Minnows.

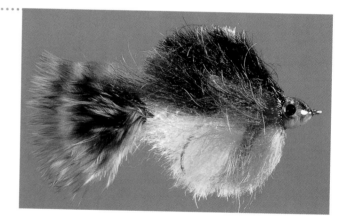

Others are Salty Minnow, Baby Rainbow, Yellow Ringed Perch, and all-black.

Dahlberg's Deep Wiggler
(Larry Dahlberg)

Hook: Tiemco 800S, sizes 2 and 8
Tail: Dubbed body segment; silicone strands
Body: Flashabou Dubbing
Legs: Silicone strands
Eyes: Epoxy molded non-toxic with black pupils
Notes: Colors include bronze, pearl, purple, black.

Subsurface Flies

Dahlberg's Flashdancer
(Larry Dahlberg)

Hook: Streamer, varied sizes
Tail: Red marabou
Body: White chenille; weighting optional
Wing: Gold Flashabou
Collar: Deer hair
Head: Spun and trimmed deer hair

Notes: Larry Dahlberg of Taylors Falls, Minnesota tied this fly in 1990. He says, "As a matter of fact, the Flashdancer preceded the Diver and it was my effort at imitating the spinner. I had an old lady that I guided that had trouble catching fish. She would make bets with the other fishermen and she would always lose. I felt terrible about it.

"She couldn't cast and it was dangerous to have her in the boat with a fly rod. I put a spinner on her line just to keep her quiet. I told her to just hold it and I would run the boat back and forth across the river. That would have worked except she kept trying to cast the spinner and endangering our lives.

"So the idea dawned on me to just tie some reflective material into the wing of a fly and see if it would go. I found that if I just tied the stuff straight on, like in the form of a Mickey Finn, it wouldn't do much. But if I tied on a Muddler-hair type head, it creates a turbulence and the wing would work real well if it was made from the right material, real thin and flexible.

"Anyway, I created this little fly and it turned into just a killer smallmouth fly. The old lady started catching sixteen to eighteen fish a day and went into the money."

When tying the Flashdancer, don't worry about a precisely trimmed Muddler-style head; in fact, leave it unruly. Those exposed hairs actually contribute to the underwater turbulence that kicks the wing into action. In this case, rough is better. Larry hasn't changed the fly over the years, except to sometimes weight it.

"I run through a spectrum of colors in some cases," Larry said, "but I mainly use gold and silver and sometimes pearl. I know guys that claim to have other-worldly experiences with all sorts of colors, but I'm not a big color experimenter.

"The Flashdancer is a real good way to pulse a system and look for aggressive fish. It's a fly that either turns a fish on or it turns a fish off and it's best used fast. It's not something you fish in a slow pool and just jig in front of them and hope they bite it. You move into riffle areas where there are lots of fish of smaller size and you can really clean up on them. You fish it in fast, riffled water, the stuff you fish a spinner in—just swing it across and they bite it.

"People write me from all over the country, that they use the Flashdancer to catch bass, trout, lakers, char, saltwater fish of various sorts—anything that eats minnows." (When I heard from him last, Larry was off to Gambia, Africa to shoot for his show on ESPN, "The Hunt For Big Fish.")

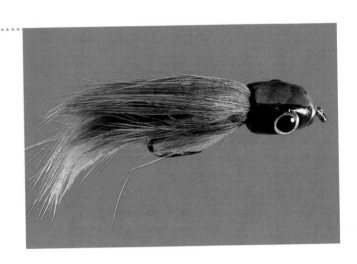

Dave's Epoxy Minnow
(Dave Rabe)

Hook: Regular shank, size 4
Tail: Short rabbit Zonker strip, olive
Collar: Rabbit strip, olive
Body: Colored epoxy

Notes: Dave Rabe of Milford, Ohio says, "When fished near the bottom this fly produces very well for me. The shape of the fly allows this fly to plane up into the water column, and with a little slack, it will drop back to the bottom, imitating a variety of sculpins."

90

Dave's Wool Minnow
(Dave Rabe)

Hook: 4x-long streamer, sizes 1/0 or 2/0
Body: Ram's wool, gray over white
Sides: Grizzly saddle hackle
Flash: Krystal Flash, pearl
Gills: Optional, red wool
Eyes: Doll or solid plastic eyes glued to lead or non-toxic barbell
Notes: Dave says, "As a larger baitfish imitation, this fly is absolutely my best producer." He also ties an olive version.

Deke's Bubble Gum Worm
(Deke Meyer)

Hook: 2x- or 3x-long hook, heavy wire (Tiemco 5262 or 5263), size 6
Thread: Fluorescent pink, heavy
Tail: Continuation of Ultra Chenille or Vernille; optional marabou tuft
Body: Fluorescent pink Ultra Chenille or Vernille, medium or large, extends over hook eye; lead wire
Rib: Wire, tinsel or sparkle material
Notes: This is a variation of Burk's V-Worm, tied as a finesse worm for smallmouth bass. For sight-fishing the Umpqua at the Big K Ranch, I tie it like a giant San Juan Worm, using just the Ultra Chenille or Vernille, without the marabou. Unlike chenille, Ultra Chenille or Vernille won't fray from the core, and is neutral-density, so the trailing ends of the material tend to float up in the water, adding lifelike movement (and you need to weight the fly to sink it). You can enlarge this fly for

largemouth (see Yamagata's Eliminator Worm). Ultra Chenille and Vernille are product names for synthetic chenille, which comes in various colors and diameters, the fattest of which works best for bass flies. Available from fly shops, including A-1 Fish Fly Fishing Supplies and The Fly Shop and wholesale from Cascade Crest Tool (see Sources, page 130).

Dusty's Mono Minnow
(Dustin Harris)

Hook: 2x- or 3x-long standard or heavy wire
Thread: 6/0, color to match body
Tail: Marabou; optional sparkle material (such as Krystal Flash, Flashabou, etc.)
Body: Dyed monofilament; clear mono over thread, floss or sparkle material (such as Krystal Flash, Flashabou, etc.)
Head: Sparkle dubbing
Eyes: Plastic barbell or burned monofilament; non-toxic mini-barbell eyes; bead head
Notes: Color schemes: olive, brown, black, yellow, white,

hot pink, hot red, chartreuse, etc. Having access to a public pond within a few miles of his home in Monmouth, Oregon, Dusty Harris can immediately run his prototype flies past an assembly of bass and bluegill.

Its slim shape suggests a minnow or fry, or possibly a damselfly nymph when dressed in tan or olive. The marabou tail imparts movement, while the dyed mono body and sparkle dubbing head suggest a life-like quality. The subdued eyes also add to the minnow/damselfly equation. (The wrapped mono body is reminiscent of the proven saltwater standard, the Glass Minnow.)

The Mono Minnow is slim, durable, easy-to-tie with readily available materials, and the fish like it. Using the size-6 Mono Minnow in light olive in the photo (notice a bit of monofilament still attached to the hook eye), Dusty nailed a nice largemouth in the pond: "My hand span is seven inches, and the bass was over three-hand-spans long, so I'm figuring about 21 or 22 inches." In these northern waters, that translates to the five- to six-pound range. And since Dusty is a catch-and-recatch fisherman, that mama is still haunting the pond.

Although you can find marabou and sparkle dubbing almost anywhere, Dusty offers all the materials needed to tie his Mono Minnow through his Body Basics (see Sources, page 130).

England's Brass Wonder
(Tim England)

Hook: Eagle Claw 214, size 6
Overwing: White marabou; pearl Krystal Flash
Underwing: Gray marabou; peacock herl
Head: Brass bead
Notes: This is the silver minnow version. The other is olive. Available from Umpqua Feather Merchants (wholesale).

Enrico's Bluegill
(Enrico Puglisi)

Hook: Mustad 80300, sizes 2 to 2/0
Thread: Clear monofilament, super fine
Underwing: Rust, yellow, eel green EP Fibers; orange
    Flashabou dubbing strands; green Flashabou; black,
    olive permanent marker
Gills: Red Krystal Flash
Wing: Eel green EP Fibers; orange Flashabou dubbing
    strands; black, olive permanent marker
Eyes: 6 mm plastic molded, black on amber
Weedguard: Mason hard mono 20-pound
Notes: EP fibers and Enrico's flies available commercially (see Sources, page 130).

Hot Bass Flies

Enrico's Yellow Perch
(Enrico Puglisi)

Hook: Mustad 80300, sizes 2 to 2/0
Thread: Clear monofilament, super fine
Underwing: Orange, yellow, white EP Fibers; orange
    Flashabou dubbing strands; green Flashabou; olive
    permanent marker
Gills: Red Krystal Flash
Wing: Olive EP Fibers; orange Flashabou dubbing
    strands; olive permanent marker
Eyes: 6 mm plastic molded, black on amber
Weedguard: Mason hard mono 20 pound
Notes: EP fibers and Enrico's flies available commercially
(see Sources, page 130).

Hanley's Tron Minnow
(Ken Hanley)

Hook: Tiemco 8089, size 6
Tail: Antron, white
Body: Antron, white
Underwing: Pearl Krystal Flash
Wing: Antron, white, gray, olive, Matuka-style
Collar: Red hackle
Head: Red wool
Weedguard: Optional, Mason hard mono 15-pound
Notes: This is the Redhead Shad version. Others include
the Panfish Haze and saltwater versions. Ken Hanley is
author of *Western Bass*, 1995, Adventures Beyond
Publications.

Harmeling's Krystal Minnow
(George Harmeling)

Hook: Tiemco 300, size 6
Tail: Frayed out Mylar tinsel, pearlescent
Body: Mylar tinsel, pearlescent
Throat: Orange grizzly hackle
Wing: Synthetic hair, yellow, olive; blue Krystal Flash;
    mallard flank
Head: White
Eyes: Painted, black on orange
Notes: George says of his fly, "At best, you might consider
calling it Harmeling's Variant. The pattern is a basic
smolt-type, based on Alaskan and blue smolt patterns.
It's probably more accurate to call it a transplanted
smolt pattern, not an original."

Hidalgo's Cupid 'Do
(Carlos Hidalgo)

Hook: Mustad 34007, size 4
Thread: Color to correspond with the color of the wing (red)
Wing: One or two different colors of Angel Hair (red)
Underwing: Angel Hair (gold)
Head: Thread (red); epoxy
Eyes: 3mm stick-on, black over fluorescent yellow
Notes: Carlos says "This is a good example of a flasher fly that I use for peacock bass. I tie it in a wide range of colors. I also tie it in three colors, for instance, green over yellow with a white under wing. Flasher patterns are flies tied entirely with flashy materials such as Flashabou, Krystal Flash, Lite Brite and the like. I like to use these types of flies on partly cloudy days when light levels vary.

The extra flash gets them noticed even when clouds are blocking the sun. They are also effective in full sunlight."

Hidalgo's Flash Minnow
(Carlos Hidalgo)

Hook: Mustad 34007, size 2
Thread: Size A chartreuse
Body: Pearl Krystal Flash; small hollow plastic tubing (or substitute monofilament, Swannundaze or Larva Lace)
Wing: Flashabou, chartreuse
Head: Chartreuse thread; epoxy
Eyes: Painted black over white
Other Colors: Yellow/orange, rainbow/blue back, white/pearl, white/green, chartreuse/green
Notes: Carlos Hidalgo of Miramar, Florida and author of *South Florida's Peacock Bass*, 1997 says "This streamer fits all the criteria of a good peacock bass fly: it is a relatively small, very colorful, and flashy baitfish imitation. I tie

this pattern to fish several south Florida lakes where there are an abundance of tiny, almost transparent, minnows that peacocks feed on, but it effective anywhere." (See Sources, page 130 for his book.)

Hidalgo's Flashy Hooker
(Carlos Hidalgo)

Hook: Mustad 34011, size 4 to 1
Thread: Fine transparent nylon thread
Weedguard: 16-pound-test Mason hard monofilament
Tail: Colorado spinner blade; split ring; barrel swivel
Body: Pearl Poly Braid, Diamond Braid or similar
Wing: Pearl Flashabou, trimmed short to avoid fouling hook
Head: Pearl Poly Braid; epoxy
Eyes: 3 mm molded prismatic adhesive, black on red
Notes: Carlos ties this fly in various colors, matching a

size-4 hook with a size-00 blade and size-14 swivel; size-2 hook with size-0 blade and size-12 swivel; size-1 hook with size-1 blade and size-10 swivel; and the smallest possible split ring on all sizes.

He says, "The Flashy Hooker came about in an attempt to create a fly with the characteristics of a spinnerbait. This pattern attracts fish in the same way as the lure does—with lots of flash and vibrations. The Hooker is very versatile. It can be fished with a steady, moderate retrieve, which really whirls the blade. It can also be retrieved with shorter, quicker strips, which I think adds more motion and flash to the wing as well as setting off a different type of vibration through the water. Another effective technique is to strip it to a drop-off and let it sink. I have taken many largemouth while the Hooker slowly helicopters to the bottom. Sometimes if a fish is following the fly, you can stop your retrieve and the sinking fly gets him to commit."

Hidalgo's Hardhead
(Carlos Hidalgo)

Hook: Mustad 34007, size 2 for peacocks; size 2 and 1 for largemouth
Tail: Blue pearl Lite Brite over white The Fuzz
Underbody: Lead wire
Body: Pearl Poly Braid, Diamond Braid or similar
Wing: White The Fuzz; blue pearl Lite Brite; white The Fuzz
Head: White chenille; epoxy, 2 coats
Eyes: 3mm silver prismatic adhesive
Other Colors: Yellow; chartreuse
Notes: Carlos says, "You can substitute another type of soft synthetic synthetic streamer hair or lamb's wool for The Fuzz. The Hardhead acts like an underwater Muddler. It attracts fish by pushing water and setting off

vibrations with its oversized head. The fly casts well, hardly ever fouls, and peacocks love it. I think that the idea of attracting fish with vibrations is often overlooked in fly fishing."

Hidalgo's Mosquito Fish
(Carlos Hidalgo)

Hook: Mustad 34007, size 4
Thread: Gray
Underwing: White bucktail
Wing: Gray bucktail; gray squirrel tail
Lateral Line: Single-strand silver Krystal Flash
Head: Gray thread; epoxy
Eyes: Painted black over white
Notes: Carlos says, "This is a very simple, yet very effective largemouth bass streamer. I tie it to imitate the mosquito fish (Gambusia) which thrive in the area, but it can also mimic any small, drab-colored minnow. Both largemouth and peacocks feed on mosquito fish, but while this fly is deadly on largemouth, it is not very

effective on peacocks—it's not colorful or flashy enough."

Hidalgo's Peacock Streamer
(Carlos Hidalgo)

Hook: Mustad 34007, size 2
Thread: Fluorescent yellow
Wing: Bucktail, yellow, orange; orange Krystal Flash; green bucktail
Head: Fluorescent yellow thread; epoxy
Eyes: Painted black over fluorescent yellow
Notes: Carlos says "This is by far and away my best peacock fly and it has also caught its share of largemouth bass." He also calls it his No Name Streamer. In his book *South Florida's Peacock Bass*, 1997 he continues, "It is easy to tie, casts beautifully, hardly ever fouls, and most importantly, catches lots of fish. Due to its streamlined shape, the fly works well with a moderate to fast retrieve. It looks like a very colorful fleeing minnow in the water, something which no self-respecting peacock could pass up. I keep about a dozen of these in my fly box; I would not think of going fishing without them.

Another good feature about the No Name is that it is a good exploring pattern that has caught just about everything that swims in the area's fresh water. Largemouth bass, bream, crappie, and baby tarpon have all fallen for it. The name, by the way, came from about a half-dozen failed attempts at a flashy moniker." (See Sources, page 130 for his book.)

Hidalgo's Son Of Hardhead
(Carlos Hidalgo)

Hook: Mustad 34007, size 2 for peacocks; size 2 to 1/0 for largemouth
Underbody: Lead wire
Body: Pearl Poly Braid, Diamond Braid or similar
Wing: Chartreuse craft fur; peacock Angel Hair
Head: Chartreuse chenille; epoxy, 2 coats
Eyes: 2.5 mm silver prismatic adhesive
Notes: Carlos says, "The Son of Hardhead is a thin-bodied version of the original Hardhead. I tie this in a lot of different colors."

Jensen's Silimander
(Milt Jensen)

Hook: Mustad 34011, sizes 1/0 and 2, bent back
Tail: Flared hackle tips; pearl Krystal Flash
Rear Collar: Purple marabou
Body: Chenille
Legs: Silicone strands
Eyes: Non-toxic dumbbell
Notes: This is the purple version. The other is chartreuse.

Kruger's Thunderspin
(Ron Kruger)

Hook: Mustad 3366, size 4
Tail: Marabou; blade and swivel
Body: Marabou
Notes: Ron Kruger of Benton, Kentucky says, "It may seem strange to some, but before the advent of spinning gear, most everyone who fished, fished with a fly rod. During the first quarter of the twentieth century, anglers used the long rod for everything.

"But the rods were large, heavy and soft. And the things they threw for bass and other warmwater species were heavy and hard to fish. So it's no surprise that when open-face spinning reels came along that the majority of fishermen drifted away from fly fishing.

"Strange how things come around. The tide has turned, and the current is drifting gradually back to the long rod and the special connection it gives us to fish— all fish.

"It might also surprise you to learn that back when everyone fly fished for smallmouth and largemouth bass, the most popular and effective fly/lure was not Peck's Popper, but a fly/spin combination.

"In fact, these old fly/spin combos looked very much like today's Roostertail and Mepps spinners. They were a simple wire with a Colorado blade that spun around the shaft of the wire. At the end of the wire was a clip, to which the fly was attached. A Woolly Worm was the most popular attachment, but many used streamers.

Fly/spin combos were difficult to cast because they were heavy, and they were almost impossible to pick up out of the water because of the drag of the spinner. Once anglers learned they could fish virtually the same thing with ease on a spinning rod, the fly/spin combo lost popularity, even though they were much more productive than poppers.

"I came up with a fly/spin combo that is slightly different than the old original, but just as productive. Years ago they didn't have the small swivels and tiny Colorado blades available now. And, instead of placing the spinner up front, where it would exert drag on the pick-up, I placed it behind the hook. Besides, it always has made more sense to me to place the flash toward the tail than toward the nose of an artificial. That's where all the action is." Available from Krugercraft (see Sources, page 130).

Lefty's Deceiver
(Lefty Kreh)

Hook: Standard length; varied sizes
Tail: Three to five pair saddle hackles; six to ten strands Krystal Flash or Flashabou each side
Collar: Bucktail or calf tail
Gills: Ten to fifteen strands red Flashabou or Krystal Flash
Topping: Peacock herl or bucktail (medium gray, light green or blue)
Eyes: Optional; painted or adhesive eyes
Weedguard: Optional
Notes: Tied in many variations, this is probably the most famous saltwater fly of all time and still accounts for as

many predator fish as any other pattern in use today. It's deadly on all species of bass.

Lynch's B'wana's Mop Fly
(Dan Lynch)

Hook: Offset shank, black-nickel worm hook (extra-wide gap); size 1/0, 3/0

Tail: Ultra-suede crayfish form

Body: Turkey feathers from duster

Weight: Lead barbell, (small, 1/36 ounce for 1/0; medium, 1/24 ounce for 3/0)

Weedguard: 20- or 25-pound-test stiff mono (4 strands 1/0, 5 strands 3/0)

Head: 5-Minute Epoxy (Devcon recommended) over eyes and chenille; extra-fine pearlescent glitter optional

Notes: Color varies (presentation more important most of the time): white, white/red, red/white, black, blue, tan, brown, etc. You could call the Mop Fly a master bass-hunter's Jig N' Pig: professional guide Dan Lynch of Ennis, Texas spends many days fishing Lake Fork Reservoir outside of Dallas, where largemouth bass grow big.

Dan says, "During the winter on Lake Fork you have to slow the fly down to a crawl—you have to fish the fly real slow, and the slower, the better. When the water temperatures are in the high 40s, low 50s, the bass's metabolism slows down, plus they go real deep.

"The fish tend to school up in the same places the same time of year, and in winter the bass don't really travel far. A lot of people think they school up and head for the deepest water they can find, and they do, but it's the closest deep water to them. They'll just submerge down; their travels in cold water are more vertical than horizontal."

Some of Dan's favorite spots are off points or in creek channels, where he concentrates on the bends. He says, "From fishing an area so much I know where the bass are going to be, but I don't know which bush they're in, so I graph these bushes in 12 to 30 feet of water, then probe for them with the fly. You have to work that fly into the submerged tree tops, bush tops and some structures we've actually placed in the water over the years."

Depending on water depth, he'll fish a floating line and watch for the line/leader junction to twitch, or he'll fish a sink-tip such as a Teeny line to get down farther. Because winter bass have slowed down, their underwater take is often subtle—so subtle that detecting a strike in 25 feet of water can be difficult.

"You're looking for one or two good bites a day," Dan says, "and that's probably all you're going to get. You might get three or four, but if you do, you're real lucky. A good bite is a big fish, ten pounds or above. Our

medium fish is five to ten pounds, but people don't get excited about them—it's the big fish we get excited about."

Dan designed the Mop Fly to sink slowly and to push a lot of water so that bass can not only see the fly, but identify it as prey with the nerves in their lateral lines. A common misconception is that the bass are on the bottom; more often they are suspended, usually in proximity to cover. So if Dan is casting to a bass holding in a tree-top at the 15 feet level in 25 feet of water, it's imperative that the fly be sinking slowly when it approaches the 15-foot mark. Another key factor is that the Mop Fly is presented in a vertical manner, not horizontally. There is no stripping or retrieving; you intensely concentrate on the line as the fly sinks, hoping to detect that subtle strike.

The Mop Fly derives its name from the turkey feathers Dan gleans from inexpensive dust mops or feather dusters commonly found at discount stores in the housewares department. (Look for dusters with turkey feathers, not saddle hackle or schlappen because they won't work well.) The turkey feathers run from two to eight inches long, so the amount you'll need per fly varies. When wrapping the feather, Dan ties in the tip and continues down into the marabou fluff, until the stem gets too big and too stiff. (The thick stem will crack and break when wrapped around the hook shank.) Short turkey is difficult to work with, but makes a durable fly.

The dusters I found were orange, yellow, pink, blue and green. When tying Mop Flies, Dan favors white, red, black, blue, red with a white head or white with a red head. When he creates the head, Dan adds epoxy paint to the 5-Minute Epoxy, making it black or red or whatever color he chooses. As an alternative, I wrap the head with chenille to gain color. Also, as the epoxy dries, Dan bends the mono weedguard to the proper angle. I prefer to lock the weedguard in place with the chenille, then apply the epoxy. As it dries, I dust the head with extra-fine pearlescent glitter to add a bit of sparkle.

Dan cuts the crayfish form from Ultrasuede, a man-made material from fabric stores that won't shrink or discolor in water or after it's dried. He believes the crayfish form attracts bass because they are an important menu item, but also because "it makes them mad".

He says, "On Lake Fork there's one area in December where the big fish will actually school on top, feeding on the big shad, usually before the sun comes up or late evening. And that's when the big white Mop Flies work well. You'll see 10- to 12-pound bass busting these shad that are 12 inches long. The Mop Fly acts like a dying shad; it sinks at about the same rate." He says there is also a jig bite during pre-spawn.

Dan says bass have a sense of smell six times more acute than ours; by putting scent on the dry ultra suede, hits to his flies go up by 40 percent. He believes the type of scent is not important—it mainly masks the human scent imparted to the fly when we touch it, in addition to masking fumes from super glue, moth balls, chemicals used in dyeing materials, head cements, etc. For more information, contact Dan Lynch (see Sources, page 130).

Lynch's B'wana's Snoz
(Dan Lynch)
Hook: Worm hook, size 5/0 to 1/0; keel style
Tail: Krystal Flash, black, red; Flashabou tubing frayed out, silver
Rattle: 3 or 4mm glass
Body: Silver Flashabou tubing; epoxy
Overbody: Continuation of tail; epoxy
Eyes: Solid plastic, black on amber
Weedguard: Strands of stiff mono
Notes: The epoxy is applied so one side is fatter than the other, causing the fly to swim erratically. The keel style has a bucktail wing to help it swim hook-point-up.

Maddin's Sean Sizzler
(Russ Maddin)
Hook: Long shank stainless, size 1/0
Tail: Purple rabbit strip
Rear Collar: Purple marabou; pearl Flashabou
Body: Purple chenille; palmered purple saddle hackle
Head: Purple chenille
Eyes: Non-toxic, black on yellow

Mallory's Shimmer Perch
(Chris Mallory)

Hook: Long-shank stainless steel, size 1/0
Underwing: Yellow Aqua Fibers
Wing: Yellow grizzly hackle; sea green Aqua Fibers
Gills: Red Aqua Fibers
Head: Gray Aqua Fibers
Eyes: Solid plastic, black on yellow
Weedguard: Mason hard mono 20-pound
Notes: This is the perch version. Others are Shimmer

Martinez Furry Leech
(Raymond Martinez)

Hook: Stinger, size 2
Tail: Furry Foam, custom dyed two-tone
Body: Angora Flash dubbing
Eyes: Nickel-plated lead
Weedguard: Maxima chameleon
Notes: This is a purple/hot pink tip version. Others include three-tone custom versions. Available at Flies By Night.

Matador; antique fly
(William Cassard)

Hook: Blind eye salmon; snelled silkworm gut leader
Tip: Fine silver round tinsel
Tag: Red floss
Butt: Peacock herl
Tail: Married swan or goose, red over yellow over black
Body: Silver flat tinsel
Wing: Barred woodduck flank feather
Hackle: Green
Head: Red wool
Notes: This Matador tied by Marvin Nolte of Bar Nunn, Wyoming is a fine example of flies used for bass in the 1800s. In her book, *Favorite Flies and Their Histories*, 1892, 1988, Mary Orvis Mayberry wrote, "This fly was designed by Mr. William J. Cassard, of New York City, and later named by C.F. Orvis the Matador; i.e., the killer. Its gay, rich dress reminds one of the picturesque matador of the Spanish bull-fights, who is also the

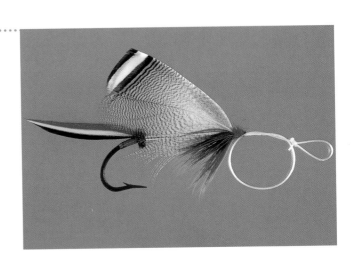

triumphant killer. Mr. Cassard has also invented two similar patterns that are excellent bass flies, which he calls the Romany Rye and Romany Ree, both having wings of the black barred wood duck, like those of the Matador." Although only a few pages relate to bass, Paul Schullery's *American Fly Fishing: A History*, 1987, is another interesting reference book.

Mihulka's Mr. Right
(Chris Mihulka)

Hook: Tiemco 205BL, size 8; Mustad 37160, sizes 4-8, front 1/4 of shank bent
Tail: Black marabou
Body: Black chenille; palmered black hackle
Legs: Black rubber
Head: Black chenille
Eyes: Painted lead or non-toxic
Notes: Chris Mihulka of Springfield, Oregon developed Mr. Right as a variation on a Woolly Bugger, retaining all its fish-pleasing characteristics, but adding some unique features. He calls it Mr. Right because it always lands right-side-up.

When fished, the fly drops through the water nose-first; when bass see the undulating marabou and hackle, they rush over and eat it as it cascades towards the bottom. When the fly is resting on the bottom, the reversed-hook and supporting "platform" of rubber legs and weighted eyes cause the marabou tail to wave like a flag, up above the rest of the fly. When a bass inhales the fly, the fish sucks in marabou and a sharp hook point because the hook bend and point are also elevated. This design is snag resistant because the hook point is up and away from the bottom.

While floating the clear waters of the Umpqua River in Oregon, Chris watches smallmouth as they inspect his fly. Often he can only see the rubber legs (which is why white, fluorescent orange, yellow and chartreuse legs are an advantage). The smallmouth will tip up slightly, nosing right up to Mr. Right, sometimes tasting the marabou, sometimes just inhaling the fly. When Chris sees the legs disappear, he sets the hook.

Chris ties Mr. Right in all-black or black with a chartreuse tail for clear water, in tan or yellow for cloudy water, and in orange or tan as a crawdad imitation. He varies the colors of the legs and eyes, but is particularly fond of chartreuse eyes.

Mr. Right is a design prototype; besides colors you can vary the materials. For example, you can substitute medium Ultra Chenille, eliminate the hackle, use four legs on each side, or use a rabbit strip for the tail.

You may not realize it, but when submerged, a rabbit-strip tail floats upwards. I was curious how Mr. Right tied with a rabbit tail would look underwater, so I tossed it into the bathtub. My wife, who was bathing at the time, did not exclaim, "Oh, Mr. Right." In fact, when I asked her what she thought of Mr. Right, she said, "Wrong—get that thing out of here!"

This approach may offend some traditionalists, but when smallmouth get finicky, I've increased my catch rate by soaking a rabbit-strip-tail Mr. Right in crawdad oil. I've watched smallmouth disdain Mr. Right, then swim downriver (downwind, so to speak) where the scent could reach them, and have them whirl around and engulf Mr. Right. It may be the wrong approach for some anglers, but, at times, for me it's the right way to fish Mr. Right. Available commercially (see Sources, page 130).

Mike's Epoxy Zonker

Hook: Stainless steel, long shank, sizes 4 and 6
Tail: White rabbit, frayed out pearl Mylar tubing
Body: Continuation of tail; epoxy
Wing: Continuation of tail
Eyes: Real eyes with adhesive insert
Notes: This is the white version. Others are black, chartreuse, olive. Available wholesale from Spirit River.

Morris Green Butt Ugly
(Mike Morris)

Hook: 2x- or 3x-long, heavy-wire, streamer hook, size 6
Thread: Black
Weight: Fifteen turns .025-inch lead wire
Butt: Fluorescent green chenille
Body: Black chenille
Legs: Fluorescent green round rubber
Notes: The water is so clear in Oregon's Umpqua River by mid-July that you can easily see smallmouth swimming among the sunken ledges and rock canyons, and with water temperatures up, the bass are on the prowl. When I first started fishing the Umpqua I caught bass by retrieving Woolly Buggers, but I've since greatly increased my catch rate by sight fishing. The trick is to cast far enough upstream for a dead-drift presentation with a weighted fly so that the fly's sink-rate will intercept the waiting smallmouth.

Retired guide Mike Morris says, "I like to use the light or bright colored legs because I'm not watching the fly, I'm watching those legs. When I cast to a fish, I'm watching the fish, I'm watching the fly, and as soon as I see those legs disappear, I set the hook. I don't wait to feel anything because most of the time you're not going to feel anything anyway.

"People that say they're not catching fish are getting a lot more hits than they realize. They're not feeling the fish, and if you can't sight-fish and see them take the fly in, you don't have any idea that they're there."

While fishing "The Loop", a ten-mile section of river only accessible via guided float trips or while staying at the Big K Ranch, Mike caught and released a male smallmouth on August 7, 1996 that measured 23 3/4 inches with a 17-inch girth, and weighed 8.2 pounds on his digital scale. He was unable to nail a female that was close to 25 inches that he estimates would go nine pounds. (The current Oregon record is a lake-caught fish of less than 8 pounds.)

Murray's Madtom Sculpin
(Harry Murray)

Hook: Streamer hook, sizes 8 to 4
Tail: Black rabbit strip
Body: Cross cut rabbit strip, trimmed
Collar: Some of the cross-cut rabbit left untrimmed
Eyes: Lead barbell
Notes: In his book *Fly Fishing for Smallmouth Bass*, 1989, Harry Murray of Edinburg, Virginia, wrote: "Mad toms come out from under the rocks at night and move about the river to feed. I have my best success fishing mad tom patterns for the first hour of daylight. After foraging for food all night they seem to be a little slow getting back under the rocks and the bass get a good shot at them.

"Water about two to three feet deep over gravel bars can be very productive. These areas can be fished from the river or the bank side. I like to cover these areas with a very slow stripping action, often wading upstream to avoid scaring the bass. I like to feel the streamer bump the bottom occasionally just to let me know I'm getting down to where the real ones are." Available from Umpqua Feather Merchants (wholesale).

Nealley's Dragon
(Alan Nealley)

Hook: Long shank size 6
Underbody: Black Antron
Body Weave: Brown Larva Lace
Wingpad: Hen pheasant hackle tip
Collar: Hen pheasant
Head: Brown Super Possum
Eyes: Black Plastic Bead
Notes: Available from Umpqua Feather Merchants (wholesale).

Nix's Sunfish
(Jimmy Nix)

Hook: Stinger, size 2
Tail: Olive hen hackle
Body: Olive wool; copper wire rib
Gills: Red marabou
Wing: Matuka-style tail continuation; olive marabou
    overwing
Cheeks: Orange wool
Collar: Olive wool
Head: Olive wool
Eyes: Lead, painted black on yellow
Weedguard: Mason hard mono 20-pound
Notes: This is the Woolhead; the other version is the

Deer-Hair. Available wholesale from Umpqua Feather Merchants.

Nixon's Calcasieu Pigboat
(Tom Nixon)

Hook: Mustad 3366, size 1/0
Body: Fat black chenille
Hackle: Black palmered
Collar: Black rubber strands
Head: Black thread
Eyes: Painted, red on yellow
Notes: Tom Nixon, of Lake Charles, Louisiana, now in his 80s, tied this fly in March, 1998, based on his pioneering book, *Fly Tying and Fly Fishing for Bass and Panfish*, 1968, 1977.

In the early fall of 1950 Tom Nixon birthed his Calcasieu Pig Boat fly (pronounced Cal-ka-shoo) on the wings of frustration. Tom says, "Living in Louisiana at the time, I fished with some of the top bait-casters in the area. They were always laughing at my fly rod bass, so I had to do something, just for my own pride. They were using the Hawaiian Wiggler, and that's where the basic idea came from. It was just a case of trying to hold my head up—I got tired of being shoved around. You know how that stuff goes."

At the time, Tom was living in Calcasieu Parish, near where the Calcasieu River flows into Lake Charles. He says, "In World War I, they called the German submarines pig boats; the Calcasieu Pig Boat is named after the river and it's an underwater killer, so it's called Pig Boat." (Of course, a common term for a hefty large-mouth is "pig", so the name is doubly appropriate.)

In a letter to me in January, 1996, Tom wrote: "We lived in deep southwest Louisiana for thirty-two years where I had the opportunity to fish with some of the country's finest bait casters. These anglers, gentlemen all, gave me and my fly rod a hard time. With better tackle, fly-rod spinnerbaits, Calcasieu Pig Boats and four-inch plastic worms I eventually was able to hold my head up when the day's sport was discussed around the camp fire.

"I even got to the point where I won a bass tournament on Toledo Bend Reservoir. It was surprising some of the names given to my tackle and also some of the places they told me to shove it. Vanquished bait casters lack charm and grace—they are definitely poor losers.

"If I'm fishing the Pig Boat, I'll fish the banks and vertical rock piles. I'll just cast up to them and just sit there for a count of 10 or 15 or 20 and let the thing settle down. Then just give it little twitches to give it some motion, and slowly bring it back." Tom uses a 10-foot sink-tip with a 7 1/2-foot leader tapered from 25-pound test to 14-pound test.

Ramsey's Estaz Worm
(Mike Ramsey)

Hook: Tiemco 8089, size 2; Mustad 3407, size 1/0
Tail: Black Estaz, spun and twisted
Body: Black Estaz
Weight: Optional non-toxic or lead wire
Eyes: Bead chain or non-toxic barbell or painted lead
Weedguard: Mason hard mono 20-pound
Notes: This is the black version. Others are chartreuse, purple. (see Sources, page 130).

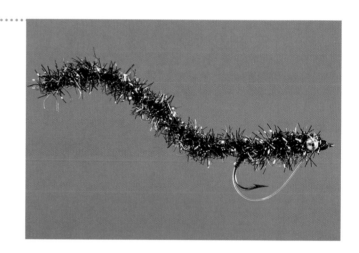

Ramsey's Glitter Bug
(Mike Ramsey)

Hook: Tiemco 200R size 4
Weight: Lead wire, 20 wraps .025
Tail: Two black round rubber strands, small
Body: Purple Estaz palmered with black hackle
Rib: Black wire
Front Legs: Two black round rubber strands, small
Notes: This is the purple version. Others are black, chartreuse, orange. (see Sources, page 130)

RAW's Flexo Lizard
(Richard A. Whitner)

Hook: Mustad wide gap, straight shank, worm hook
Thread: Fine clear mono
Tail: Marabou or Fly Tails by Wapsi (Cabela's)
Body: Shaped 1/8- or 1/4-inch Flexo tubing; colored with
    permanent marker
Legs: Latex or Fly Tails threaded through tubing
Eyes: Molded eyes by Witchcraft or Orvis
Weedguard: Wire double loops, bent
Notes: Richard also uses a hookless version, with a short
length of clear plastic tubing inserted and glued in the
lizard nose, which allows you to change fly bodies with-
out re-tying a new hook.

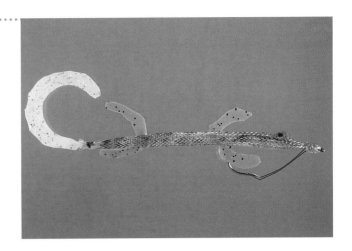

RAW's Gitzit
(Richard A. Whitner)

Hook: Straight eye, long shank, wide gap
Thread: Clear mono thread, fine
Tail: Sili Legs, varied colors
Body: Flexo tubing
Underbody: Ice Chenille
Weight: Lead barbell on top of hook shank
Notes: Richard says, "This fly is like the lures that the
pros use, like the Gitzit or the G2 used by Shaw Grigsby.
It's fished on the bottom in a hopping motion. It can
also be stuffed with Alka Seltzer to leave a trail of bub-
bles, or you can insert a rattle in the body for sound in
dingy water."

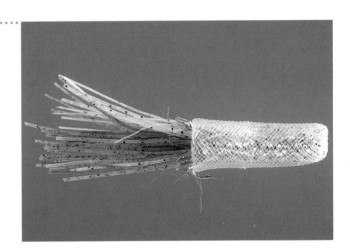

RAW's Magna Herring
(Richard A. Whitner)

Hook: Wide-gap, bent-shank, worm hook; sizes 5/0 to 1
Internal Head: Clear plastic tubing, short length
Body: Flexo tubing inverted over itself, tied off, shaped
    into triangular shape
Tail: Optional, marabou or Flexo extended and frayed out
Notes: Flexo can be colored with permanent markers.
Richard says, "This fly was designed after the soft jerk
baits used by tournament bass fishermen like Shaw
Grigsby. This fly should be fished at various depths from
the top to the bottom. You can use a faster, erratic
retrieve to keep it right on the top or it can be slowed
down to dive slightly or left to sit, then fished in a slow,
erratic retrieve to fish deeper.

    "Lead or non-toxic wire can be wrapped around the

hook shank to get it down quicker. The hook comes in
and out of this bait to change colors quickly and effi-
ciently. You can slide a rattle in through the walls of the
fly, which rides hook-point-up, keeping it fairly snag
proof." Available from Orvis.

Ryan's Epoxy Baby Bass
(Thomas C. Ryan, Jr.)

Hook: Long shank streamer, size 8
Tail: Olive marabou; Krystal Flash, green, gold
Body: Krystal Flash dubbed (tail colors), pulled over
body; 5-minute Epoxy
Eyes: Adhesive, black on gold

Ryan's Krystal Flash Shad/Baitfish
(Thomas C. Ryan, Jr.)

Hook: TMC Stinger 8089, size 2
Tail: Krystal Flash, black, pink, pearl
Body: Goop or 5-Minute Epoxy
Eyes: Doll or solid plastic
Notes: Tom varies the sink rate with the body finish and
the eyes.

Ryan's Sparkle Grub
(Will Ryan)

Hook: Standard, varied sizes
Tail: Chartreuse marabou; chartreuse Krystal Flash
Body: Chartreuse Estaz
Eyes: Non-toxic, red on black, on top of shank, cement-
ed with Super Glue
Notes: Will Ryan of Florence, Massachusetts says chartreuse seems to work in all water stains and he likes it
on a size-1/0 worm hook. Other colors include white;
yellow/brown; black; purple. Body can be weighted with
lead or non-toxic wire.

In his book *Smallmouth Strategies for the Fly Rod*, 1996,
Will wrote, "The fuzzy glow resembles very closely the
tube jig's fluorescence, and the weighted head, marabou
tail, and glittery Flashabou do their best to keep up with
its flash and action. The fly capitalizes on the tube jig's
best features—bottom presentation, tubular shape, and
soft texture—and the smallmouth's inexplicable attrac-
tion to fluorescent chartreuse.

"While this fly produces in smaller, shallower waters,
it is especially valuable in lakes, reservoirs, and navigable
rivers. Here is where the jig fishers have always had it

over the fly fishers; here is where this fly closes the gap.

"Whether drifting or anchored or, for that matter,
fishing upstream in current, fish Sparkle Grubs and similar patterns as you would a jig. Bass often take on the
drop, so watch the line carefully as the fly settles to the
bottom. Once it hits the bottom, retrieve it in 3- to 4-
inch strips, with the rod pointed right at the spot where
the line enters the water. Keep the strips sharp, but not
in rapid succession.

"Pull the line over your index finger on the hand
holding the rod. Rather than pinch the line as you

would on a standard retrieve, let it slide back over your finger a little. This enhances the hopping motion of the fly while keeping the overall retrieve slow. You often set the hook inadvertently on the retrieve."

Fly fishing for smallmouth dates back over 200 years; Will wrote, "In 1785 one Robert Hunter Jr., a visitor to the area around Montreal, described in his diary the excellent angling in the nearby rivers. It was nothing, apparently, to fly fishermen to catch three dozen fish in a half hour. Smallmouth bass, that is.

"Although smallmouths were noted in a report on the St. Lawrence valley written in 1664 as well as in a Jesuit's account of the Great Lakes in 1761, Hunter's diary entry is the first mention of fly fishing for them."

Ryan's Wiggle-Hex
(Thomas C. Ryan, Jr.)

Hook: Long-shank streamer hook, size 8; rear, straight-eye, long-shank hook with bend and point cut off
Tail: Mallard dyed wood duck, 3 sections
Rear Body: Pale olive rabbit dubbing, marabou for gills, brown raffia shellback, silver wire rib
Front Body: Hinge, Duramax; pale olive rabbit dubbing picked out on sides, brown raffia shellback, silver wire rib
Legs: Dark brown soft hackle or schlappen
Eyes: Black mono
Notes: Tom says, "Magnum-size deadly on pond bass."

Sanchez Conehead the Barbarian
(Scott Sanchez)

Hook: Dai-Riki 930 stainless; Mustad 3366, size 2
Thread: 3/0 red
Body: None
Wing: Synthetic wing material, white, blue, chartreuse; silver holographic strands; pearl Krystal Flash
Head: Tungsten bead; prism tape; epoxy
Eyes: Adhesive, black on yellow
Notes: Scott Sanchez of Livingston, Montana says, "Conehead the Barbarian combines the features of some very effective fly patterns with a new concept to create a productive new multi-species pattern. I came up with this fly while living in Austin, Texas and enjoying the excellent fresh and saltwater fishing Texas has to offer.

"The Clouser Minnow is an effective pattern for about any fish that swims. Lead-eye flies dive to the bottom quickly and have a vertical jigging motion that seems to attract and entice fish. However, these eyes can pick up vegetation and are prone to being hung up on substrata when fishing riprap or rocky areas. The eyes will lodge in the cracks and may require you to rerig your tackle during a feeding frenzy.

"Bendbacks are also an effective streamer pattern. The Bendback hook design is very snag-resistant without the use of weedguard. They work great in shallow

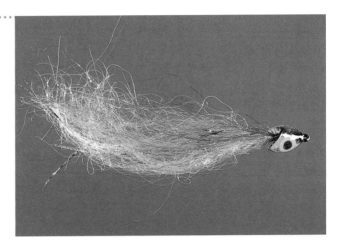

water and with sinking lines in deeper water, but even when weighted with lead wire they won't have as pronounced of a jigging motion as a Clouser. It made sense to combine the attributes of these two flies.

"Metal beads were a logical choice for the weighted head of the fly. I've used standard, round, fly tying beads on small bendbacks with good results. On larger sizes they just don't look quite right. The Conehead bead seems to give a better profile and many times can be coaxed out of the rocks when hung up. I've painted the Coneheads like a jig head and covered them with Mylar tubing.

"Wrapping the Coneheads with prism tape provides the best results. It forms a great minnow head and you get some bonus gills in the process. The prism tape is available from Witchcraft Tape products and comes in numerous colors. There are metallic colors, fluorescent shades, pearlescent and glow-in-the-dark tapes, which are extensively used in the lure industry and are also sold in fly shops. Other waterproof tape options are duct tape and electrician's tape, which can be purchased in many colors. I overcoat the tape head with epoxy to make it more durable.

"This fly can be tied in numerous sizes and colors, and existing patterns can be adapted to this style. Bucktail or calf tail are used on most of my flies, but hackle, rabbit, synthetic hair and marabou also work well.

"It was originally fished for white bass, black bass and stripers, with enthusiastic approval. It's also proven its worth in the salt and is my favored fly for catching flounder. It has accounted for over twenty species."

Sanchez Double Bunny
(Scott Sanchez)

Hook: Dai-Riki 930 stainless, size 1/0 to 3/0
Thread: 3/0
Body/Wing: Two rabbit strips, darker on top, lighter on bottom; contact cement (VAL-A brand latex)
Flash/Lateral Line: Krystal Flash or Flashabou
Underbody: .035 lead wire wrapped around front half of hook
Head: Fletch-Tite vinyl archery cement or epoxy
Eyes: 5/16 adhesive, black on yellow
Weedguard: Mason hard mono 20-pound
Notes: Scott says, "The Double Bunny is my favorite big-fish fly. It brings out some of the fish you don't usually see. The idea for the Double Bunny came to me on a fishing trip to Belize eleven years ago. John Hanlon and I were trying to catch some barracuda that were not being cooperative. The two flies that ended up working the best were a Kiwi Muddler and a FisHair 'cuda fly. I thought, What if you could put together the pulsating action of rabbit fur together with the undulating action of a 'cuda fly? Add in the profile of a large baitfish and you would have a fly that looked alive in the water. I didn't have the necessary materials to tie the Double Bunny on that trip so it had to wait for later.

"The following couple of summers found me observing large trout trying to eat smaller fish on the end of my line, so the idea came back to me of the Super Barracuda fly and the first Double Bunny came out of the vise. The first time I fished it, the mackinaw and cutthroat below Jackson Lake on the Snake River seem to really want to eat it. It would pull the fish out of

nowhere. I've used it successfully ever since. It's a great fly for finding and catching large fish.

"So far it's caught cutthroat, rainbows, hybrids, browns, brookies and mackinaw. On the non-trout list, there are snappers, groupers, tuna, mackerel, jacks, 'cudas, tarpon, salmon, stripers, pike, largemouth bass, smallmouth bass, a bluegill over three pounds and even a catch-and-release, fly-rod record, channel catfish. The 1992, 1993 and 1994 Jackson Hole One-Fly contests were won on Double Bunny variations.

"For bass fishing, I have had good results fishing the Double Bunnies in shoreline structure with a floating line. I prefer a fast retrieve for this. I also use it with sinking lines over deeper habitat. With the action of the rabbit, this fly can be fished slowly if the fish are less active and it has action when it is dropping. When you encounter bass or stripers schooling on top, cast and let it sink below the frenzy. By doing this you can pick up larger fish that are suspended and picking up the scraps." Marketed by Dan Bailey (see Sources, page 130).

Sanchez Lipstick Minnow
(Scott Sanchez)

Hook: Mustad 34011, size 2
Tail: Gray marabou or rabbit hair
Tube Holder: Pearl or silver Mylar braid
Underbody: Rainbow Krystal Flash; silver Brighton
Overbody: 1/8-inch ID x 3/16-inch OD clear vinyl tubing
Head: Epoxy
Eyes: Adhesive, black on red
Weedguard: Mason hard mono 20-pound

Notes: Scott says, "The Lipstick Minnow came out of a need to have a small, translucent minnow that was quick to tie and still had a translucent, epoxy-type look. While in the hardware store, I say some clear vinyl tubing that looked like it might do the trick.

"I tied a few and since Jackson, Wyoming is a little far from the ocean, the original test drive was on the Snake River. I had a 19-inch mackinaw eat the Lipstick Minnow. It has since been tested on tunny, bonefish, sea trout, redfish, jacks and a variety of other smaller inshore species. Bass, crappie and sunfish eat it, too.

"It's an excellent fly to fish at night around lighted docks. With a weedguard, it can be fished on flats or in vegetation. The original fly had a hot glue head, but now I use epoxy. If you don't want to use epoxy, solid plastic eyes can be put on with Aquaseal or Goop."

Incidentally, the names derives from Larry Sutherland of the Austin Anglers shop, who thought the fly looked like a transparent tube of red lipstick with a bit of the lipstick showing on the end.

Sanchez Lounge Lizard
(Scott Sanchez)

Hook: Black up-eye salmon, size 2 to 3/0
Thread: Fluorescent red 3/0
Body: Black rabbit strip; silicone caulking, glitter; impale the hook point through it
Legs: Three stands black rubber each side
Throat: Fluorescent red chenille
Head: Black Conehead

Notes: Scott says, "This fly is a variation on the standard Sluggo Fly (see Sanchez Sluggo and Sluggo Leech below). It is a little less snag resistant, but it will sink quicker and doesn't require carrying hooks with you. The sinking rate of the fly can be controlled by using different sized Coneheads or using tungsten cones for extra weight. I also tie it with plastic beads for a lightly weighted fly. Heart-shaped Pony craft beads make a

great-looking head. Tie it with or without rubber legs. Spandex legs work very well on smaller flies and will have more action on the drop." Marketed by Dan Bailey as Black Lizard (see Sources, page 130).

Sanchez Sluggo
(Scott Sanchez)

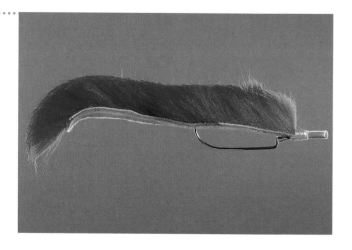

Hook: Offset shank worm hook, size 1/0

Body/Tail: Rabbit strip; silicone caulking; glitter; impale the hook point through it

Legs: Optional

Head: Vinyl tubing, 3/16 inch

Notes: Scott says, "The Sluggo Fly came about as a way to fish for bass in heavy cover. Some very popular and effective lures for large bass are the soft plastic baits. A friend of mine, Bill Jones, is a partner in a great bass lease-lake in East Texas. He needed a fly to compete with his fishing partners, who were doing very well with large plastic worms and Sluggos. These baits have a soft feel to them, fish very well on the drop and work well on finicky bass in all water depths. They are also very weedless.

"I worked on a few prototypes and sent them to Bill. I used some on the local cutthroat trout, too. These originals were tied Bendback-style with a rabbit strip. They definitely worked but needed some fine-tuning.

"I decided to tie it as a tube fly. This way you could rig it like a Texas-Rig Worm. I found that the rabbit strip needed a little more body to keep the hook in it while casting so I put a little clear silicone caulking on the belly of a rabbit hide along with some glitter in it. The coated rabbit looks sexy and the soft feel convinces the bass to hold onto it longer. This arrangement is much easier to get hookups with than the usual mono weed guard. Since takes can be subtle, this is very important."

"The early test runs with this were great. Along with Bill Jones and Robert Cathey, I used them to catch some very nice fish in heavy cover and over deeper grass flats. I threw them onto lily pads, hopped them off and pull them up on the next pad. We fished them on floating, intermediate and heavy-sinking lines and caught fish at all depths. This fly fishes very well on the drop and with slow retrieves."

"These flies have been fished for smallmouth and stripers with good results and I've caught some monster sunfish with them too. Pike eat them and since they are quick to tie—who cares if they ruin them. The silicone treatment also adds to the durability of the fly. They also work very well with a wad of rubber legs tied onto the head. This gives it the lizard look. This fly can also be used in salt water—it is a good, snag-resistant fly to throw in the grass and mangroves.

"This fly can be tied in about any color; my favorites are black, purple, chartreuse and rust. I often use fluorescent colored thread on the head to give a firehead look. Rubber legs can be tied in matching or brightly contrasting colors. This fly can be fished large or small and can used for any fish species where you need a fly that can fished slow through cover.

"This fly is much easier to tie with a vise for tube flies. Or you can make a simple adapter out of a bicycle spoke. Cut the spoke off about an inch-and-a-half from the nipple end. File the sides of the unthreaded part so they are flat. This will allow your vise to clamp the spoke tight. Screw the spoke nipple on to the spoke so that the large end of the nipple goes on first. Use 3/16" vinyl tubing available at aquarium shops and hardware stores for the tube."

Author's note: Besides whole rabbit skins, from Dan Bailey's (and other fly shops) you can get magnum rabbit strips, 1/4 inch wide. I cut a slit in a foam-core sheet (you can use cardboard but it bends too easily). With a large-diameter-needle bodkin, I work the rabbit fur into the slit so that just the skin is showing, then pin the hide in place. I use a jumbo craft-toothpick to apply automotive/marine silicone (it has UV inhibitors so it withstands exposure to sunlight), then sprinkle extra-fine pearlescent glitter over the silicone before it dries. (The foam-core sheet, jumbo toothpicks and glitter available in arts and crafts supplies.)

You can add a "hot tip" to the strip by gluing a contrasting color to the end, such as a short bit of fluorescent chartreuse rabbit strip added to black, glued hide-to-hide, then add silicone and glitter to the rest of the strip. Scott uses contact cement; I use the same silicone used to reinforce the rabbit hide.

If you wish to incorporate more flash, before you apply silicone to the rabbit hide, sew in strands of sparkle material (Flashabou, Krystal Flash, etc.) with a large needle, threaded with a bobbin threader. Or make a small slit in the hide, insert a crochet hook, Cortland line splicing tool or Rainy's E-Z Leg Tool in the slit, then pull the sparkle material through the hide.

Sanchez Sluggo Leech
(Scott Sanchez)

Hook: Mustad 3366 bent into bendback, sizes 4 to 8
Thread: Olive 3/0
Body: Olive rabbit strip; silicone caulking; glitter; impale the hook point through it
Head: Conehead or bead
Notes: Scott says, "This is a smaller version of my bass Sluggo fly. The bendback design allows it to fished through the weeds without hanging up. This puts it in the proximity of fish and helps to prevent spooking them. It is important to lightly coat the back of the rabbit hide with silicone caulking. This will reinforce the

hide to prevent the hook from pulling out. Other good colors are black, rust, tan and purple."

Scheck's Bass Roach
(Art Scheck)

Hook: Mustad 3366 or other straight-eye, sizes 4 on up
Thread: Black 6/0 or 8/0
Tail: Three or four grizzly hackles per side, concave side facing in; silver Flashabou
Body: Silver Mylar tinsel
Collar: Natural squirrel tail
Head: Black thread
Eyes: Painted, black on white; epoxy head
Notes: Art says, "This is a version of the Cockroach tarpon fly. I have no idea why bass find it appealing, but they do. There doesn't seem to be any particular circumstance in which it works best. I use it as a desperation fly when the bass are uncommonly moody and

have refused flies that make sense. I have my best luck with small sizes (2 and 4)."

Scheck's Concealed Weapon
(Art Scheck)

Hook: Mustad worm hook, 33645, (has a bent shank), sizes 2 or 1/0
Thread: Gray 6/0 or 8/0
Tail: Olive over white marabou; silver Flashabou
Weight: Lead wire strips tied to hook underside
Body: Red floss
Underwing: White craft fur, sparse
Sides: White craft fur, sparse; pearlescent Krystal Flash
Head: Darken top of head, permanent marker; clear nail polish
Eyes: Painted, black on yellow; epoxy head
Wing: White calf tail, squirrel tail

Notes: You can use any color combination you want for the Concealed Weapon, which is designed to float hook-point-up. Art says, "The two strips of lead wire attached to the underside of the hook (the side opposite the point) act as a keel of sorts. I like to use craft fur for the bottom half of the collar because it sinks very well, and the calf tail/squirrel tail for the top of the collar because the natural hair retains air bubbles when it hits the water (at least for a second or two), which makes the top of the fly more buoyant than the bottom and helps it assume the proper attitude. These flies almost always swim point-up."

Scheck's Crafty Minnow
(Art Scheck)
Hook: Mustad 33620, sizes 2, 4 and 6
Thread: Gray 6/o or 8/o
Body: Pearlescent Mylar tinsel
Rib: Oval or round silver tinsel
Belly: Craft fur, silver-gray, white
Wing: Craft fur, silver-gray, tan, brown; pearlescent Flashabou
Gills: Red craft fur or floss
Head: Darken top of head, brown permanent marker; clear nail polish
Eyes: Painted, black on yellow; epoxy head
Notes: Art says, "Craft fur can be purchased at craft, sewing, and department stores. It doesn't retain air when it hits the water, which makes it sink quickly, but it doesn't soak up water, either, which makes it pleasant to cast. You can throw a pretty big Crafty Minnow with a 4- or 5-weight outfit. Since the fibers are the same diam-

eter form end to end, there's no need to attach precise lengths of material to the hook; just lash it all on and trim it to length when you're done. In the water, craft fur has more movement that natural hair, isn't as floppy as marabou, and reflects light nicely. It's my favorite material for small baitfish patterns. You can tie this fly with whatever colors of craft fur you find, but this pattern has been very good for me."

Scheck's Marabou Deceiver
(Art Scheck)
Hook: Heavy, straight-eye (Daiichi J141), sizes 4 on up
Thread: Gray 6/o or 8/o; weedguard with 3/o white Monocord
Tail: Full white marabou blood feather, sparse gray or tan marabou; silver Flashabou, 8-12 strands each side
Body: Silver Mylar tinsel
Collar: White calf tail; pearl Krystal Flash on sides
Wing: White calf tail; natural squirrel tail
Throat: Red craft fur
Head: Darken top of head, brown permanent marker; clear nail polish
Eyes: Painted, black on yellow (nail polish); epoxy head
Notes: Art says, "Deceiver-type flies are exceptionally reliable bass lures. I substitute marabou for the standard saddle-hackle tail because marabou has more action, particularly on a slow retrieve, and I replace the peacock-herl topping with squirrel tail for the sake of durability. You could tie this fly in various colors to match local baitfish, but I generally stick with a simple dark-over-light pattern." Art is the former editor of *Fly Tyer* magazine.

Smith's Ultra Minnow
(Capt. Briant Smith)

Hook: Standard, size 1/0 to 4/0

Body: Olive Ultra Hair

Wing: Olive Ultra Hair; olive or pearlescent Krystal Hair on sides of wing

Cheeks: Ultra Hair, yellow, orange

Head: Marine Goop (has added sun-damage inhibitors)

Eyes: Solid plastic, black on yellow

Notes: This is the bream version, with black, vertical bars made with a permanent marker. Others are white with gray back, a shad imitation; white with chartreuse. Captain Briant Smith of Lake Charles, Louisiana, prefers Ultra Hair, but if it's not available, you can substitute other translucent synthetics. To get the final streamlined shape, he places the fly under the hot water faucet, which causes the hair to sweep back, making it sleek and aerodynamic.

Briant guides anglers for redfish, spotted sea-trout and offshore species. He says, "I wanted something that was real streamlined and easy to throw and more of a fish appearance to it. All predatory fish eat smaller baitfish; matching a baitfish is not as easy as one may think. Most of them are translucent or almost transparent. It's important that you use the clear, and not the opaque white, Ultra hair. You want this stuff to disappear in the water and it does. It's very durable material, lasts forever, doesn't rot—it's nylon, and it's easy to work with.

"My original fly was developed for stripers because of the small shad they were feeding on. I kept working on the pattern until it ended up as it is now. Then I started fishing them offshore, and found that Spanish mackerel, bonito (little tunny), cobia, shark, everything I threw it to, hit it. So I started working on different color combinations, and the more I played with the fly, the more I realized that this thing is, in fact, an ultra fly because it's so versatile. You can color it with marking pens in the field, you can trim it in the field to match a specific baitfish profile—short, fat, long, skinny or whatever. I've imitated menhaden (pogie fish), cacohoe (killifish),

mullet. So far I've taken 13 species of fish with it, both fresh water and salt water."

The innovative aspect of the Ultra Minnow is the way Briant folds the synthetic hair back on itself, creating the simulation of the baitfish's body, but without bulk. In essence, the fish's belly is similar to an upside down Matuka, High-Tie or Blockbuster. The strands of hair that encompass the hook point deflect weeds on the retrieve.

Briant says the biggest mistake tiers make is to use too much material, making it difficult to work with. So the idea is to use sparse bunches of hair, with only a few strands of sparkle material along the sides of the wing.

Briant says, "If it's white, it's right; if it's chartreuse, fish don't get loose." He uses a variation with blended blue tones for the back, with translucent light blue topped with translucent dark blue or purple (very sparse amounts of hair), but his favorite is white and chartreuse.

Another variation is to use colored thread instead of white. For instance, in some glass minnows you can see their internal organs, suggested with red or orange thread. Also, you can tie the white/chartreuse version with chartreuse, olive or dark green thread. If you're fishing and you notice the fish are taking 1 1/2-inch minnows, you can trim your fly to size. To get the maximum action from the Ultra Minnow, Briant fishes the fly tied to the tippet with an open loop knot.

Spirit River's Beadhead Firecracker
(Spirit River)

Hook: Stinger, size 6
Legs: Glitter Leggs
Wing: Marabou, red, white
Head: Lite Brite; gold bead, counter drilled
Notes: This are six versions available wholesale from Spirit River.

Spirit River's Big Eye Hot Tail Bonker
(Spirit River)

Hook: Long shank, stainless steel, 2 and 6
Tail: Rabbit strip, purple tipped with fluorescent chartreuse; peacock black Holographic Mylar Motion
Collar: Purple rabbit
Body: Purple Estaz
Legs: Glitter Leggs
Eyes: Deep See Aluminum Eyes, black, with 3-D molded stick-on inserts, black on yellow

Spirit River's Conehead Bonker
(Spirit River)

Hook: Stinger, 2 and 6
Tail: Rabbit strip, chartreuse; silver Holographic Mylar Motion
Collar: Chartreuse rabbit
Body: Chartreuse Estaz
Legs: Rubber, hot chartreuse
Head: Cone, gold
Weedguard: Double hard mono loops
Notes: This is the chartreuse version. Others are black, purple, white, olive. Available wholesale from Spirit River.

Spirit River's Woolly Bomber
(Spirit River)

Hook: Long shank, 2 and 6
Tail: Marabou, silver Holographic Mylar Motion
Body: Chenille palmered with black hackle; side stripe continuation of silver Holographic Mylar Motion
Head: Brite Blend, chartreuse
Eyes: Real Eyes with adhesive insert
Notes: This is the olive/black version. Others are all black, black with chartreuse head, black with hot red head. Available wholesale from Spirit River.

Stewart's Fuzzy Wuzzy
(Jim Stewart)

Hook: Stinger, size 2
Tail: Krystal Flash; long, soft hair
Butt: Red yarn
Legs: Rubber strands
Rear Wing: Red Krystal Flash
Collar: Hair or wool
Head: Thread
Eyes: Large round silver
Weedguard: Double hard mono
Notes: This is the yellow/white version. Others include red shad; purple shad; black, gray. Jim Stewart ties for collectors (see Sources).

Sublett's Lead-eye Sculpin
(Randy Sublett)

Hook: Long shank, size 6
Tail: Tan rabbit strip
Body: Gray yarn
Pectoral Fins: Tan rabbit strip
Wing: Tan rabbit strip
Collar: Brown deer hair
Head: Deer hair, white, brown, black, olive
Eyes: Nickel-plated lead

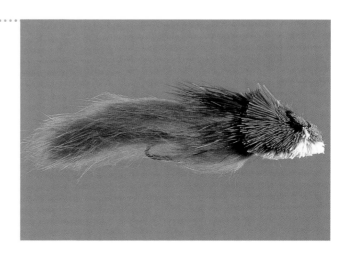

Sublett's Lead-eye Shad
(Randy Sublett)

Hook: Mustad 3407, size 2/0
Tail: Marabou, white, gray; silver Flashabou
Body: Deer hair, white, gray, black, in wedge shape
Eyes: Nickel-plated lead

Sublett's Sparkle Minnow
(Randy Sublett)

Hook: Mustad 3407, size 2/0
Underwing: White bucktail
Overwing: Red bucktail
Head: Epoxy over rod winding thread; glitter
Eyes: Solid plastic, black on orange
Weedguard: Mason hard mono 20-pound

Swisher's Devil Leech
(Doug Swisher)

Hook: Stainless, long shank, size 1/0
Tail: Tasmanian devil hair, black; black Krystal Flash
Body: Mohlon, black
Wing: Tasmanian Devil Hair, black; black Krystal Flash
Notes: This is the black version. Others are pink/white, yellow/white, white, olive, brown. Available from Doug Swisher.

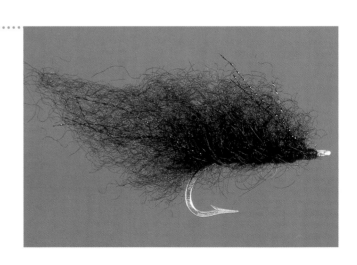

Tamboles Beaded Beauty
(John Tamboles)

Hook: Stinger or streamer, size 6

Thread: Danville's Fly Master Plus, fluorescent chartreuse or orange

Tail: Fluorescent yellow marabou; 5 strands yellow or
pearl Krystal Flash

Body: Fluorescent yellow plastic beads; fluorescent
orange chenille

Notes: Also in olive and fire tiger, especially for peacock
bass. Available from Fantastic Flies (see Sources, page
130).

Tamboles Pee-Wee
(John Tamboles)

Hook: Mustad 3407, size 6 or 4

Tail: Loop of monofilament securing Curly Tail screw
lock; Mister Twister Curly Tail, chartreuse

Body: Rear, chartreuse Estaz; front, orange Estaz

Eyes: Medium Real Eyes with molded adhesive inserts

Weedguard: Mason hard mono 20-pound, one strand, end
flattened

Notes: John Tamboles of Cooper City, Florida catches
largemouth and peacock as well as redfish with this fly.
Available from Fantastic Flies (see Sources, page 130).
(See also Walega's Crazy Eight.)

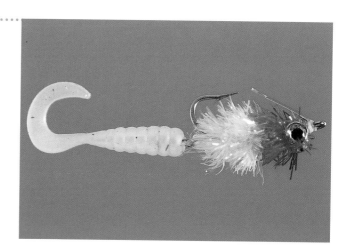

Traditional Spinner/Fly

Hook: Various

Tail: Spinner; wire loop

Body: Various; white chenille; white hackle

Weedguard: Wire

Notes: This traditional spinner/fly combo was rendered
by Ron Knight of Leavenworth, Kansas, who combined
the traditional Woolly Worm with a spinner. In his
book, *The Fly Rod for Bass*, 1925, Cal Johnson wrote, "A
spinner used in connection with a bass fly will add to
the effectiveness of the lure, especially on dark days.
Single spinners of about sizes 1 to 2 work very well on
the ordinary bass fly tied to a number 4, or larger, hook.
The double spinners will be found better adapted to the
flies of large size, say 1/0 or 2/0, for example. Pearl spinners are used by many anglers when the waters are roily
or darkened from heavy rains, as their whitish body can
be seen from some distance."

Traditionally, fly rod spinner/fly combos were the

norm—cast with cane rods with lengths of 12 to 15 feet.

In his *Book of the Black Bass*, 1881, 1923, James
Henshall wrote, "The most commonly used artificial
bait for black bass is the spoon-bait or trolling-spoon.
It is now made in all shapes and many sizes; but all are
made upon the same general principle, and are merely
variations of the original trolling spoon, which was

fashioned from the bowl of a spoon, a single hook being soldered to one end, and a hole drilled in the other end for attaching the line.

"This rude device was first used for pickerel fishing on the lakes of central New York. It was then improved and patented by Julio T. Buel. His improvement consisted in causing the spoon to revolve on the elongated shank of the hook.

"John J. Hildebrant, of Logansport, Indiana, was the first to make any real improvement on the old Buel spoon. Instead of following the old plan of causing the

spoon to revolve on the shank of a hook by a simple hole in one of its ends, or by means of a small metal loop or ring soldered on, he substituted a small U-shaped clevis or flat swivel to slide on the stem or shank, to which the spoon was attached."

On a package of Hildebrant spinners purchased in 1999, it says: "The first Hildebrant Spinners was made from a dime and a hairpin in 1899." A rarity in the twenty-first century, after a hundred years, they are still made in Logansport, Indiana; the smaller blades in oo and o work well with flies.

Tullis Weedless Leech
(Larry Tullis)

Hook: Long shank, sizes 2/o to 8
Thread: 3/o, color may match or vary
Tail: Marabou; sparkle material optional
Body: Larva Lace tubing
Wing: Marabou inserted into Larva Lace; sparkle material optional
Head: Thread
Eyes: Nickel-plated lead barbell; optional, painted with T-shirt fabric paint
Notes: Earth tones, fluorescent colors (Larva Lace comes in 14 colors). A newer design from Larry Tullis of Taylorsville, Utah, the small plastic tube of Larva Lace offers a more flexible body/weedguard—an advantage for light-biting fish. Placed at a 45-degree angle, the tube stops just short of the hook point, acting as a weedguard.

Larry says, "Usually when I'm fishing it slow through

the weed beds the fish would hit it light—sometimes it would almost feel like you were pulling off a stick or something, but there would be a fish there when you set up. In more open water, along the outside of weed beds, the fish would hit it real hard, like they were coming out of the weeds and grabbing it, then turning to go back in the weeds."

Tullis Weedless Minnow
(Larry Tullis)

Hook: Long shank, sizes 2/o to 8
Thread: 3/o, color may match or vary
Tail: Marabou; sparkle material optional
Body: Closed-cell foam cylinder
Wing: Grizzly hackle tips; sparkle material optional
Head: Sparkle chenille (such as Glo-Brite or Crystal Chenille)
Eyes: Nickel-plated lead barbell; optional, painted with T-shirt fabric paint
Colors: Vary, such as white, yellow, chartreuse, etc.
Similar to the Weedless Leech but with barring from dyed grizzly hackle.

Tullis Weedless Woolly Bugger
(Larry Tullis)

Hook: Long shank, sizes 2/0 to 8

Thread: 3/0, color may match or vary

Tail: Marabou; sparkle material optional

Body: Closed-cell foam cylinder

Hackle: Palmered saddle

Head: Thread

Eyes: Nickel-plated lead barbell; optional, painted with T-shirt (fabric paint)

Notes: Colors vary, such as black, white, yellow, chartreuse, etc. Available from Larry Tullis (see Sources, page 130)

Walega's M.R. Crazy Eight
(Michael R. Walega)

Hook: Mustad 3366, size 2

Tail: Two Fly Tails, small

Body: Chartreuse Vernille

Wing: Glimmer

Head: Chartreuse Vernille

Eyes: Nickel-plated lead

Notes: This is the chartreuse version. The white does not have the wing. Mike gets the Fly Tails from Cabela's and they are available in larger sizes. To tie them in properly: when the fly is laying flat on its back, with the lead eyes on the bottom, hook point up, the Fly Tails are horizontal, parallel with the lead eyes. The Fly Tails flare to

each side, forming an "8" pattern that drives bass crazy with its wiggling, undulating action (see Sources, page 130).

Walega's M.R. Leech
(Michael R. Walega)

Hook: Mustad keel, size 2

Body: Black vernille

Wing: Black rabbit strip super glued to weedguard

Collar: Black rabbit fur (spun in loop)

Head: Dubbed black rabbit

Eyes: Lead or nickel-plated dumbbell

Weedguard: Heavy black mono or guitar string

Notes: Mike Walega of Commerce Township, Michigan designed his fly to incorporate a nylon guitar string that stiffens the rabbit strip to form a weed guard. This clever wing/weed guard will lessen snag-ups, but you'll still sacrifice flies, especially since this leech is destined for bottom bouncing with a jig-like action. But since this fly is quick and inexpensive to tie, you won't be

emotionally involved if you lose it in sunken structure. Mike ties his leech in black on a size-2 Keel Hook, though you could go with other colors and sizes. Available through Michael R. Walega, M.R. Flies (see Sources, page 130).

Wallace's Purple 'lectric Eelworm
(Jon Wallace)
Hook: Long-shank black, sizes 1/0 and 4
Tail: Purple saddle hackle
Body: Purple Crystal Chenille
Eyes: Lead eyes painted black on hot pink
Weedguard: Mason hard mono 20-pound
Notes: This is the purple version. Others are black, chartreuse, blue, red.

Waterman's Silver Outcast
(Ralph Daugherty)
Hook: Various, standard fresh or saltwater streamer hook
Body: Silver braid
Wing: White bucktail; yellow bucktail; peacock herl
Cheeks: Jungle cock
Head: Black thread
Eyes: Jungle cock feather functions as eyes
Notes: Charley Waterman has popularized this fly through his writing, crafting stories about he and his wife Debbie (who does most of the tying) catching diverse fish in tremendously varied locales with the Silver Outcast. In the letter he sent with this fly in May, 1994 Charley wrote, "This Silver Outcast is a rather small one. Debbie ties some really big ones for salt water. Some are bushy and some skimpy like this one. This one worked for schooling bigmouths."

Charley told me this story about his coming across this streamer, some 25 years ago: "Rocky Weinstein was guiding Ralph Daugherty, a retired doctor from New England, down in the Everglades. I met them in a boat in a narrow creek and Daugherty said this fly had been working well on snook, and he gave me the streamer. Later on, I caught some big trout in Montana, and Dan Bailey, who was in the tying business, asked me what I caught the trout on, and I said I caught them on a Silver Doctor. He looked at the thing and he said, that's not the way we tie Silver Doctors. Of course, what he meant was, the materials weren't the same, and I started calling it the Silver Outcast after that. It's a good streamer and it's caught all kinds of fish; it's actually a simplified Silver Doctor. I don't know whether it was Daugherty or Weinstein that tied the thing, but apparently they didn't have all the materials for a Silver Doctor and that's the way it came out."

In his book *Fly Rodding for Bass*, 1989, Charley wrote,

"Few of our favorite streamers are chosen through true tests and I'm afraid we pick the ones that look the prettiest to us. My own first choice is what I call a Silver Outcast. It's a rather simplified form of the Silver Doctor with some strands of peacock herl that run full length and suggest a baitfish's lateral line. A few glitter strands help, too, and if I had only one streamer the Outcast would be it."

In his book *Black Bass & the Fly Rod*, 1993, Charley wrote, "I guess my favorite streamer is the Silver Outcast, which is a modified form of the ancient Silver Doctor and has changed with the addition and subtraction of various things through the years. I certainly didn't invent it, although I chose the name when the late Dan Bailey said the streamer I was using, which I thought was a Silver Doctor, didn't look like any Silver Doctor he ever produced at his fly shop. The Outcast just developed on its own. It has a white, blue, and yellow bucktail wing; a silver Mylar body; and wing topping of peacock herl, which makes a fishy streak down the side as the streamer travels. I like it tied pretty skimpily, and it casts easily, looking like no baitfish in particular and a lot of them in general. It takes no master craftsman to produce it."

Weedless Leech
(Steve Shiba/Larry Tullis)
Hook: Daiichi 2461, size 2-2/0
Tail: Foam tube; black marabou; pearl Krystal Flash
Collar: Black marabou
Head: Black Crystal Chenille
Eyes: Nickel-plated lead
Weedguard: The foam in the tail, cocked at a 45-degree angle
Notes: Various colors, purple, yellow, chartreuse, white, etc. Larry Tullis of Taylorsville, Utah says, "I never really liked the regular weed guards. They seem to miss a lot of hook-ups. I was trying to find a better system, using different shapes of wire, and then I started using the body itself as the weed guard."

For several years Tullis worked with the late Steve

Shiba in the early 90s, developing Edge Water's Weedless Leech. Available through Edge Water or Larry Tullis (see Sources, page 130).

Whitlock's Eelworm Streamer
(Dave Whitlock)
Hook: Tiemco 7999, sizes 1/0 and 4
Tail: Black saddle hackle
Body: Black dubbing or yarn; palmered with black hackle
Eyes: Silver bead chain
Weedguard: Mason hard mono 20-pound
Notes: This is the black version. The other color is purple. Available wholesale from Umpqua Feather Merchants.

Whitlock's Hare Grub
(Dave Whitlock)
Hook: Stinger, size 2
Tail: Purple rabbit strip
Body: Rabbit strips glued together, purple
Legs: Rubber, white, purple; Krystal Flash, red, purple
Eyes: Lead painted red on white
Weedguard: Mason hard mono 20-pound, double loops
Notes: This is the purple version. Other colors include black, chartreuse, motor oil. Available from Umpqua Feather Merchants (wholesale).

Whitlock's Hare Jig
(Dave Whitlock)

Hook: Stinger, size 2
Tail: White rabbit strip
Body: Rabbit strips glued together, white
Legs: Rubber, white, red; Krystal Flash, red, pearl
Eyes: Lead painted black on white
Weedguard: Mason hard mono 20-pound, double loops
Notes: This is the white version. Other colors include black/chartreuse, black/red. Available from Umpqua Feather Merchants (wholesale).

Whitlock's Sheep, Deep
(Dave Whitlock)

Hook: Tiemco 9395, bent, sizes 2 and 6
Wing: Icelandic sheep, white, yellow, gray; Krystal Flash, pearl, pearl blue, peacock; grizzly hackle; pearlescent Mylar; mallard breast feather
Gills: Red wool
Eyes: Silver bead chain or lead with black painted pupil
Notes: This is the crappie version. Others include bluegill, shad. Closely associated are swimming and waking versions. Available wholesale from Umpqua Feather Merchants.

Woolly Crawler
(Joe Ellis)

Hook: Ring-eye hook (also called straight eye)
Tail: Hot chartreuse marabou
Body: Three segments, green/black variegated chenille palmered with hot chartreuse grizzly hackle
Rattle: In rear and front segments
Eyes: Painted lead eyes, black on white
Weedguard: Mason hard mono 20-pound
Notes: Joe's fly is based on the Double Jointed Fly Worm with interchangeable Fly Worm Tail for the rear segment

Wyatt's Bluegill Hi-Tie
(Eddie Wyatt)

Hook: Tiemco 511S, size 6
Tail: Clear Super Hair
Body: Pearl Sparkle Braid
Wing: Matuka style, alternating bands of olive and tan craft fur
Throat: Craft fur, white over yellow over gold
Eyes: Hologram, black on pearl
Notes: Permanent marker: black behind eye, green in

front of eye and on underside of thread whip-finish. Eddie Wyatt of Johnson City, Tennessee says, "If I throw out and I'm popping-bugging for bluegill and one of the big old largemouth tries to get my bluegill, I'll use it. If it's hot summertime, sometimes I'll work it around the islands and stuff. And a lot of times the big old largemouth are waiting. Same way with the Golden Shiner Jerk Fly. (See Wyatt's Yellow Perch Jerk Fly next page).

"I've always said there's a tradeoff between fly rods and spinning rods. After spinning-rod fishing for so many years, what I found out was when you throw a quarter-ounce or eighth-ounce lure, a worm with a lead head, or something like that out there, you feel it—it's transmitted back to you immediately. So when a fish gets hold of it, he's going to turn loose of it because he can feel that weight. But with a fly rod, you've delivered something that's pretty much weightless. You don't feel it as quick, but he doesn't turn loose of it as quick, either.

"You point your rod towards it, and when you feel the strike or you feel something that feels kind of dead on the end—something may be pulling and maybe not— you swing your rod and pull your line at the same time, but you always point towards it. That's the secret—and you don't miss nearly as many fish."

Wyatt's Hook-Up Hellgrammite
(Eddie Wyatt)

Hook: Tiemco 5262, size 2 or 4, bent keel style
Thread: Danville flat black waxed nylon
Tail: Black rabbit fur strip
Eyes: Lead barbell, medium (7/32) or large (8/32)
Body: Spun black rabbit fur; trimmed flat on belly, slightly round on top
Wingcase: Black Swiss straw
Pincers: Rabbit fur, spin with fingers, rub in cement
Notes: Eddie Wyatt of Johnson City, Tennessee also ties a

Wyatt's Rattle Shad
(Eddie Wyatt)

Hook: Tiemco 5262, size 2 or 4
Tail: Dyed brown arctic fox
Underbody: Rattle; .035 lead wire, Zap Cat super glue
Body: Large pearl Mylar tubing
Wing: Three strands silver, three strands pearl Krystal Flash; then eyes; then white and brown dyed arctic fox
Gills: Red permanent marker
Eyes: Fused-bead gold plastic eyes (craft store, little weight because tied on top of hook)
Notes: With black permanent marker, place spot on body, behind eyes; make end of eyes black. Eddie also ties a

Rattle Rainbow Trout, both of which available from Umpqua Feather Merchants (wholesale).

Wyatt's Yellow Perch Jerk Fly
(Eddie Wyatt)

Hook: TMC 8089NP or 811S, size 10
Thread: 6/0 white
Body: Pearl Sparkle Braid
Wing: Yellow craft fur; brown permanent marker; Bondtite glue from nose to back of hook, pinched with finger
Gills: Red permanent marker
Eyes: Stick-on hologram, black on yellow
Notes: Finally, apply Softex or epoxy from nose to back of hook. (Bondtite is an archery cement for fletching arrows.) Eddie Wyatt of Johnson City, Tennessee also ties Golden Shiner, Rainbow Trout and Shad Jerk flies. Eddie says, "First thing, I wanted something that worked good that was really simple to tie. And I wanted something that suspended and didn't sink real quick.

"In lakes especially, these shad are kicking off and dying. What we're able to do with a fly rod is deliver

something out there that doesn't have much weight, and let it kick off and die like a real shad would do. And that's what these things do, they're literally jerkbaits.

"I sight-fish it—I'm watching fish most of the time when they get it, and they'll grab it and turn and go down, and that's when I set the hook. That's a really good fly—that thing looks like a fish."

Wyatt's Zonker Worm
(Eddie Wyatt)

Hook: Tiemco 8089NP, size 6
Tail: Purple Krystal Flash
Weight: Lead wire, six to ten turns, .035 inch diameter
Body: Purple Sparkle Chenille
Wing: Purple chinchilla
Collar: Teal flank feather
Weedguard: Mason hard mono 20-pound
Notes: Of his fly designs Eddie says, "What you end up with is a game plan. You end up with a plan from the top, middle, on down a little deeper, then right on the bottom. The most important thing you need to know if you're bass fishing in a lake is how deep they are. If you

don't know where they are, you're not going to catch them."

Yamagata's Bass Eel
(Jeff Yamagata)

Hook: TMC 8089, sizes 2-10
Tail: Ultra Chenille twisted with Crystal Chenille
Tail Tip: Sheep fleece or marabou
Body: Mylar tubing; black permanent marker or paint; epoxy
Eyes: Solid plastic, black on white
Weedguard: 20- to 30-pound hard Mason
Notes: This is the gray version. Other colors include olive, black, white. You can also use the Tiemco 811S hook. Available at A-1 Fish Fly Fishing Supplies.

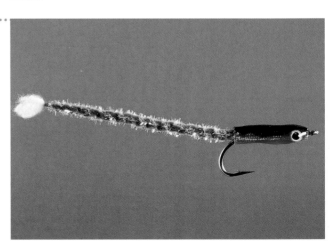

Yamagata's Eliminator Worm
(Jeff Yamagata)

Hook: TMC 8089, sizes 2-10
Tail: Ultra Chenille twisted with Crystal Chenille
Tail Tip: Sheep fleece or marabou
Body: Angora goat dubbing mixed with Lite Brite
Head: Gold, copper, silver or black bead
Weedguard: 20- to 30-pound hard Mason
Notes: When tying a worm fly, the idea is to create a limber, light fly that looks alive. To meet this challenge, Jeff Yamagata of Oakland, California developed his twisted-tail worm fly. He chose Ultra Chenille for the tail material because it's stiff enough to maintain a tail-like shape, then he adds Crystal Chenille for sparkle.

He puts those synthetic chenilles in the vise, then rotates the vise jaws to twist the two materials together. When twisted, the tail will eventually twist back on itself. When that happens, clever Jeff inserts a small clump of marabou or sheep fleece for a fish-attracting tip, not unlike the "hot tip" in a plastic worm. Then he continues twisting the tail materials until the tail reaches the proper length, then ties it to the hook. (Start with chenille length about three times desired tail length; if your vise doesn't rotate, you can use hackle pliers to spin chenille clamped in vise; when tail removed from vise, use hackle pliers, clothes pin or large office clip to keep tail from untwisting; tie down tail tuft with thread; see my article in *Fly Tying* magazine, Summer 1997.)

Jeff ties them from two to three inches for smallmouth, and up to nine inches for largemouth. So far, he's caught fish up to six pounds with his Eliminator Worm.

Jeff says, "With this fly, I usually fish a floating line, around structure—I cast into the structure, and let the fly sink, and it sinks at a fairly slow rate. Once it hits bottom, just give it a slow, varying retrieve, kind of twitching it back. For deeper water, you want to use a fast-sink tip or full-sinking line."

This is the rust version. Other colors include olive, purple, brown, chartreuse. Available at A-1 Fish Fly Fishing Supplies (see Sources, page 130).

Yamagata's Epoxy Threadfin Shad
(Jeff Yamagata)

Hook: Tiemco 811S or Daiichi 2456, sizes 6-2/0
Tail: Two to six white neck feathers
Belly: White Polar Aire or Z-lon
Back: Chartreuse Krystal Flash; white or gray Polar Aire or Z-lon; peacock herl
Head: Mylar tubing or E-Z Body over dubbed Angel Hair; permanent marker, darken dorsal area, add gills or bleeding effect; 5-Minute Epoxy
Eyes: White plastic or stick-on

Guide "Bass On Fly" Paul Hendriks has hooked Australian native bass to 12 pounds.

Hot Bass Flies

Chapter 8

Australian Native Bass

Australian native bass thrive in fresh and saltine estuary rivers and lakes, and can weigh into the double digits.

awn. Early March Down Under, calm air, warm but heading towards hot. Poppers plop down on the acre-wide, mildly swirling eddy where the Colo River joins the Hawkesbury River, about an hour and a half west of Sydney. Guide Paul Hendriks and I work the foam line of intersecting currents, experimenting with retrieves. Foot-long, silver-sided mullet burst into the air, but not for poppers. These are not game fish; Paul says you can catch them, but it's a lot of trouble because they don't readily take flies. When they bust the water, it's distracting.

Concentrating on our poppers, we are zoned in on the bass. Every so often, a vigorous boil or quick surface swirl advertises bass on the hunt. We try to cover the bass-bulge, but because the area is so huge, inevitably we are out of position or the fish is too far away. Eventually, we do catch bass, though, strong-fighting, pound to pound-and-a-half, saltwater-honed, native Australian bass. Resembling an unlikely cross between an American largemouth bass and a crappie, with a crappie's spines on the gill plates and pectoral fins, these bass put a deep bend in a 6-weight rod.

Paul tells me that his bass spawn in salt water, in the tidal portion of the Hawkesbury River, from April to September. Not all at once; nature spreads out the spawning to increase the odds for survival. Interestingly, the bass must have salt water to float its free-drift eggs—in fresh water the eggs would sink to the bottom.

After releasing another one-pound bass, Paul pours a hot cup of tea from his vacuum bottle and tells me about bassing on Lake Glenbawn, about three hours north of Sydney. He was told the bass there wouldn't take flies, so he took his 8-weight and some Dahlberg Divers to find out. Unfortunately, Paul was undergunned. Bass to 12 pounds tore him up. (He says the yellow belly, a golden perch that lives there, gets to 30 pounds.)

Now Paul quietly maneuvers his 5.2-meter (18-foot) bass boat with either the electric motor or 70 hp 4-stroke outboard up the Colo River, where we work the banks and likely structure. Eucalyptus trees host black cockatoo, who scold us and each other with loud, parrot-like screeches. From its cover in dense brush, the eastern whipbird lets loose an explosive whipcrack of sound.

Paul says the black cockatoos are his weather barometer: when they gather along the river, it means a weather change is coming. Today, however, it's hot and humid. I remove the leg portions of my zip-off pants; Paul wears shorts and is barefoot.

Cicadas add a strident zing to the air while an osprey flies over us. Although colored about the same, the Australian osprey is much bulkier than the American version. A bird about the size of a jay, the kookaburra bounces its maniacal, crazed-laughter off the trees.
Paul says, "Watch this."

He flips his popper up against the shore, along a rock ledge. A two-foot-long black lizard jumps off the rock and onto the water, charging the popper. As Paul retrieves the fly, the reptile hops across the water, snapping its mouth wide open. We clearly see the bright red cavern of its mouth as it tries to eat the popper.

I tell Paul to catch it—it would make a great photo—but he declines. "They have lots of sharp teeth and can be bloody hard to release, I'll tell you."

I envision photos of Paul trying to evict the popper from that bright red mouth amid the slashing teeth while trying to control a squirming, irate, 24-inch water monitor.

As we work up the Colo River, we cast our topwater bugs under low-hanging branches. Paul shows me his Down Under cast." He throws a tight loop up and back, then pulls it down low on the forward stroke, dipping his

body to further drop the cast. The low forward arc flips the popper under the greenery, right into bass alley.

I hunker down to try it, then realize I have been using a similar cast for years, although I hadn't realized it was an official cast. At home, a friend and I fish from his platform boat made from three hot-water tanks that were sealed, then welded to a metal frame. The

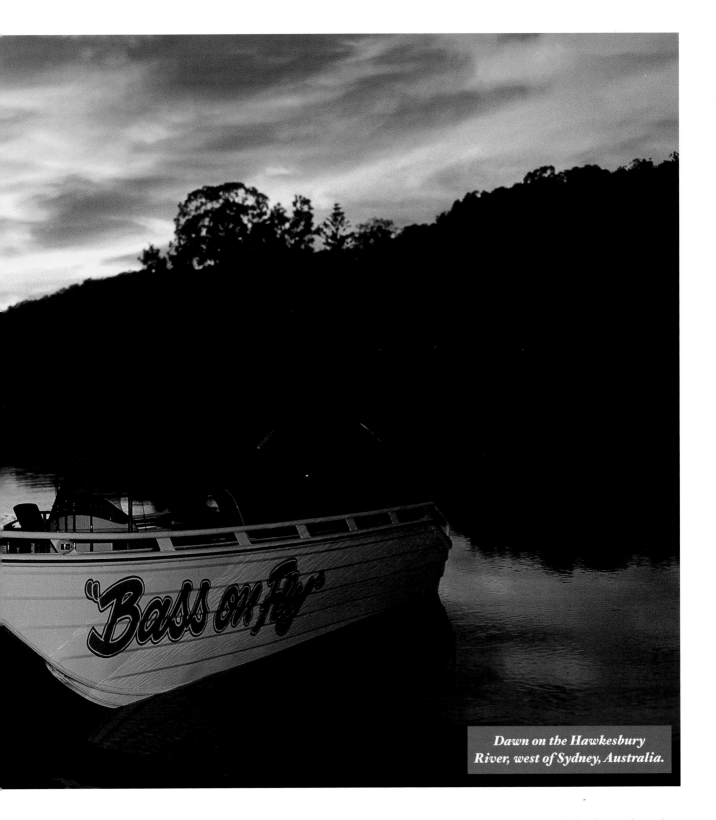

Dawn on the Hawkesbury River, west of Sydney, Australia.

boat is finished off with a plywood floor, metal railing and electric motor. While running the motor, my friend casts from a lawn chair. From that position, he is only a couple of feet off the water, so he can slip his casts under obstructions. I stand while casting, so to compensate, I hunker over a bit, then execute what I found out is Paul's Down Under cast. By any name, it works.

We never did tangle with any of the bigger bass, but since we both missed strikes, we could have missed a chunky fish. Paul showed me a photo of a Japanese client with a big smile on her face, a spinning rod, and a five-pounder. As hard as the pound-and-a-half fish fought, I suspect I might not have landed a five-pounder on a 6-weight rod. Further research is in order.

A-1 Fish Fly Fishing Supplies
Jeff Yamagata
517 8th St.
Oakland, CA 94607
(510) 832-0731

Accardo/Peck's Poppers
(wholesale only)
3708 Conrad Drive
Baton Rogue, LA 70805
(225) 355-0863
FAX (225) 355-0420

Dan Bailey
209 West Park St.
PO Box 1019
Livingston, MT 59047
800-356-4052
(406) 222-1673
FAX (406) 222-8450
www.dan-bailey.com

Bass Pro Shops
2500 E. Kearney
Springfield, MO 65898-0123
1-800-BASSPRO (227-7776)
FAX 1-800-566-4600
www.basspro.com

Cabela's
One Cabela Drive
Sidney, NE 69160-9555
1-800-237-4444
FAX 1-800-496-6329
www.cabelas.com

Cascade Crest Tool
13290 Table Rock Road
Central Point, OR 97502
(wholesale only)
800-528-0001

Bob Clouser
Clouser's Fly Shop
101 Ulrich St.
Middletown, PA 17057
(717) 944-6541

EdgeWater
35 North 1000 West
Clearfield, UT 84015
1-800-584-7647
FAX 801-825-0624
Wholesale and Retail, flies, kits
and foam
www.FishTheEdge.com
edgewater@fishtheedge

Fantastic Flies
John Tamboles
11594 SW 51st St.
Cooper City, FL 33330
(954) 989-2414

The Fly Shop
4140 Churn Creek Road
Redding, CA 96002
1-800-669-3474
(916) 222-3555
FAX (916) 222-3572

The Gaines Company
(wholesale only)
PO Box 35, Route 349
Gaines, PA 16921
(814) 435-2332
FAX (814) 435-3474

Dustin Harris
Body Basics
(wholesale and retail)
177 Cottonwood Court
Monmouth, OR 97361
(503) 838-4457

Chris Helm
Whitetail Fly Tieing Supplies
7060 Whitetail Court
Toledo, OH 43617
(419) 474-2348
FAX (419) 474-2348
(wholesale and retail)

Carlos Hidalgo
Catfish Books, Inc.
10245 SW 20th St.
Miramar, FL 33025
(954) 430-8811
E-mail: CatFishBk@aol.com

Milt Jensen
Merganser Outfitters
PO Box 45
Chico, CA 95927
Phone/FAX (530) 343-4071
Mobile (530) 520-4667

Ron Kruger
Krugercraft
14022 US Hwy. 68 EAST
Benton, KY 42025
1-800-847-4075

Dan Lynch
B'wana's Guide Service
PO Box 356
Ennis, TX 75120
(888) 667-3591

Raymond Martinez
Flies By Night
1015 B ST.
Hayward, CA 94541
(510) 538-3861

Renny Mason Company
Aerofly
4239 Chico Way, NW
Bremerton, WA 98312
(360) 377-7644
FAX (360) 792-1108
wholesale and retail

Dave McMillan
Sport Tapes
PO Box 100054
Fort Worth, TX 76185
(817) 738-3112

Chris Mihulka's Flies
(retail and wholesale)
Northwest Ties
44115 McKenzie Hwy.
Leaburg, OR 97489
1-800-334-8437
FAX (541) 896-3906

Orvis
Customer Service Center
1711 Blue Hills Drive
Roanoke, VA 24012-8613
1-800-548-9548
www.orvis.com

Dick Pobst
Thornapple Orvis Shop
Thornapple Village, Box 133
Ada, MI 49301
(616) 676-0177

Enrico Puglisi
(wholesale only)
55 West Hills Road
Huntington Station, NY 11746
(631) 427-2387
FAX (631) 427-2575

Mike Ramsey's Flies
Anglers & Archery Outfitters
136B Eden Way
Branson, MO 65616
(417) 335-4635

Spirit River
(wholesale only)
423 Winchester Street
Roseburg, OR 97470
1-800-444-6916
FAX 1-800-550-6916
E-mail: sri@rosenet.net

Jim Stewart's
Designer Flies
1104 S. Dunbar Avenue
Tampa, FL 33629
(813) 287-2761
(Custom flies by the dozen)

Mark Sturtevant
Falling Spring Outfitters
3813 Old Main Street
PO Box 35
Scotland, PA 17254
(717) 263-7811

Doug Swisher
29 San Remo Circle
Naples, FL 34112
(941) 793-7438

Larry Tullis
2588 So. 900 E. #17
Salt Lake City, UT 84106
(801) 463-9010
Wholesale and retail; flies, kits and
foam

Vann Earhart
Ultimate Poppers
(wholesale only)
PO Box 864
Ringold, GA 30736
1-800-962-8357
(706) 965-2288
FAX (706) 965-6146

Umpqua Feather Merchants
(wholesale only)
17537 N. Umpqua Hwy.
PO Box 700
Glide, OR 97443
1-800-322-3218
FAX (541) 496-3687

Michael R. Walega
M.R. Flies
6141 Brockway
Commerce Township, MI 48382
(248) 363-2604
wholesale and retail

While fishing with their brown version of a Meyer's Bead Head Rubber Legs, Bruce Olson of Umpqua Feather Merchants caught a smallmouth on the Umpqua River that he estimated went over six pounds.

When fly-fishing for bass, it's often a problem of presentation first, then fly pattern. Armed with flies the experts use, and their proven tactics, you'll be prepared to catch bass almost anywhere.

Hot Bass Flies

Deke Meyer has earned a degree in education, taught fifth graders, worked as an Experimental Biologist Aide I on the Deschutes River for the Oregon Department of Fish & Wildlife, demonstrated fly-tying and fishing all over the West at sportsman's shows, trade shows and club meetings, written columns for newspapers and magazines, and has lived the joys and frustrations of fly-fishing from the arid to the tropic, the calm to the wind-blown, on foot and via almost all types of watercraft.

His articles have been featured in most of the major fly-fishing and outdoor magazines. This is his twelfth book. Meyer is a full-time writer from Monmouth, Oregon, where he lives with his wife Barbara, who also fly fishes.

If you have any comments or would like to write to the author, he can be reached through the publisher:

Deke Meyer
c/o Frank Amato Publications
PO Box 82112
Portland, OR 97282

Other Books by Deke Meyer

SB: $9.95
ISBN: 1-878175-87-4

SB: $9.95
ISBN: 1-57188-262-6

SB: $9.95
ISBN: 1-878175-40-8

SB: $9.95
ISBN: 1-57188-066-6

SB: $24.95
ISBN: 1-57188-020-8

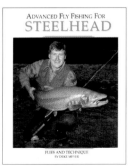

SB: $29.95
ISBN: 1-878175-10-6

SB: $15.95
ISBN: 1-57188-053-4

More Excellent Fly-tying and Fly-fishing Books!

TYING BASS FLIES: 12 OF THE BEST
Deke Meyer

Over 80 crisp, colorful step-by-step photographs show you how to tie 12 of the very best bass flies that will produce in all parts of the country. Concise tying information with fishing tips woven in, make this tying book extremely valuable for aspiring bass fly fishers. 8 1/2 x 11 inches, 32 pages.
SB: $9.95
ISBN: 1-57188-041-0

LARGEMOUTH BASS FLY-FISHING
Beyond the Basics
Terry and Roxanne Wilson

Largemouth bass are capable of jerking the rod from your hands if you're unprepared for the strike. In this book, the Wilsons discuss: understanding bass habitat; approach, delivery, and fly animation; fishing the shallows; the vertical drop; fishing the mid-depths; going deep; time, weather, and locational patterns; plus seasonal and night fishing information; fly patterns; and more. This book will show you how to catch more of these fast, powerful, acrobatic fish. 6 x 9 inches, 160 pages.
SB: $16.00
ISBN: 1-57188-215-4

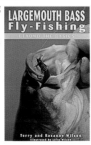

WHAT FISH SEE
Dr. Colin Kageyama, O.D.

An in-depth examination by Dr. Colin Kageyama of how and what fish see. This important book will help all anglers to design better flies and lures by its explanation of the physical processes of light in water and consequently how colors change and are perceived by fish in varying conditions of depth, turbidity, and light. Excellent illustrations by Vic Erickson and color plates that show startling color changes. This book will change the way you fish! 5 1/2 x 8 1/2 inches, 184 pages.
SB: $19.95
ISBN: 1-57188-140-9

OZARKS BLUE-RIBBON TROUT STREAMS
Danny Hicks

Ozark streams are exceptionally rich in nutrients that create big trout, Danny Hicks provides detailed information on this region's great fishing. Hicks includes: fish species, primary trout foods, all the different waters you'll encounter in the region, productive techniques for the Ozarks, fly choice, best approaches, equipment, weather, access, and more. 8 1/2 x 11 inches, 88 pages.
SB: $19.95
ISBN: 1-57188-163-8

THE ART OF TYING THE BASS FLY
Skip Morris

Skip covers: essential techniques, floating and sunk flies, divers, insects and crustaceans, pan-fish flies, plus the tools and materials you'll need for both. Bass flies are very popular for many reasons—they are durable, and fun and challenging to tie. 8 1/2 x 11 inches, 88 pages.
SPIRAL SB: $29.95
ISBN: 1-57188-076-3

GREAT SMOKY MOUNTAINS NATIONAL PARK ANGLER'S COMPANION:
Complete fishing guide to America's most popular national park
Ian Rutter

The weather, geology, geographic location, entomology, native plant life, and fisheries management policies have all combined to create daunting obstacles for the Great Smoky Mountain fly-angler. Now, Ian Rutter unlocks the secrets of this region, including: trout streams, game fish, fishing methods, fishing seasons, catching larger trout, trout flies, and more. Some of the streams are closed to fishing, but the ones open to fishing are described individually. 8 1/2 x 11 inches, 64 pages.
SB: $16.95
ISBN: 1-57188-241-3

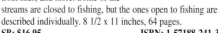

THE FLY TIER'S BENCHSIDE REFERENCE TO TECHNIQUES AND DRESSING STYLES
Ted Leeson and Jim Schollmeyer

This book features over 3,000 color photographs and over 400,000 words describing and showing, step-by-step, hundreds of fly-tying techniques! Leeson and Schollmeyer have collaborated to produce this masterful volume which will be the standard fly-tying reference book. All color, 8 1/2 by 11 inches, 464 pages, over 3,000 color photographs, index, hardbound with dust jacket.
HB: $100.00
ISBN: 1-57188-126-3
CD: $59.95 FOR PC OR MAC
ISBN: 1-57188-259-6

BLUEGILL FLY FISHING & FLIES
Roxanne and Terry Wilson

A bluegill's yanking, diving, twisting battles make for a tenacious opponent, especially on ultralight equipment. The Wilsons share: proper equipment; best flies, including their recipes and techniques for using them; identifying productive bluegill waters; bluegill habits and behaviors; effective presentations; and many more tips. 6 x 9 inches, 151 pages.
SB: $16.95
ISBN: 1-57188-176-X

FLOAT TUBE FLY FISHING
Deke Meyer

How to buy a quality float tube and miscellaneous equipment. How to operate it safely. Fly-fishing equipment and clothing recommendations. Productive fly patterns and float tube positioning strategy for best results for trout, large and smallmouth bass, and panfish. Successful strategies for fishing any lake. Illustrated, 5 1/2 x 8 1/2 inches, 125 pages.
SB: $11.95
ISBN: 0-936608-71-4

HAIR-HACKLE TYING TECHNIQUES & FLY PATTERNS
Laird Gordon Mackenzie of Redcastle

Create durable, effective, and attractive flies with the information in *Hair-Hackle Tying Methods*. Hair hackles can be used in your trout, steelhead, salmon, bass, and saltwater fly patterns. You will be very pleased with the look of the finished flies and how the hair increases the breathability and lifelike movement in the water. Full color, 8 1/2 x 11 inches, 88 pages
SB: $22.00
ISBN: 1-57188-268-5
Spiral HB: $35.00
ISBN: 1-57188-229-4

HOW FISH WORK
Dr. Tom Sholseth

Sholseth discusses: what is "scientific angling"?; angler characteristics; the aquatic environment in which they fish; equipment; effect of different kinds of light on fish; their senses and behaviors; the predator/prey relationship; strike responses; handling fish; creating a field guide; how the placement of your lure or fly looks to the fish; how to design more effective fly patterns; everything you need to understand and appreciate the species for which you fish. 8 1/2 x 11, inches, 80 pages.
SB: $19.95
ISBN: 1-57188-239-1

READING WATER
Darrell Mulch

Understanding water currents and how different flies react to them is at the heart of fly fishing. In this very thoughtful book, Darrell Mulch presents his ideas concerning fly types and water dynamics and how you should approach the stream. His drawings are extremely helpful for anglers wanting to know more about recognizing and approaching the different lies fish prefer. 8 1/2 x 11 inches, 64 pages all-color.
SB: $15.00
ISBN: 1-57188-256-1

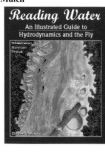

Ask for these books at your local fishing or book store or order from:
1-800-541-9498 (8 to 5 P.S.T.) • www.amatobooks.com
Frank Amato Publications, Inc. • P.O. Box 82112 • Portland, Oregon 97282